GREAT DECISIONS 2013

About the cover

Workers dismantle a euro sculpture at a terminal of the airport in Frankfurt am Main, Germany, August 16, 2012.

Photo Credit:
©Fredrik von Erichsen/ dpa/Corbis

About the back cover

The inscription is a quotation Henrik Ibsen's *An Enemy of the People* (1882), Act I, translated by R. Farquharson Sharp.

The image, which depicts the USS *Constitution*, is a reproduction of a period painting in the collection of the National Archives in College Park, MD.

PRINTED IN THE UNITED STATES OF AMERICA BY DARTMOUTH PRINTING COMPANY, HANOVER, NH.

LIBRARY OF CONGRESS CONTROL NUMBER: 2012953721
ISBN: 978-0-87124-241-9

FOREIGN POLICY ASSOCIATION
★★★★★ 1918 ★★★★★

Researched as of November 21, 2012. The authors are responsible for factual accuracy and for the views expressed.
FPA itself takes no position on issues of U.S. foreign policy.

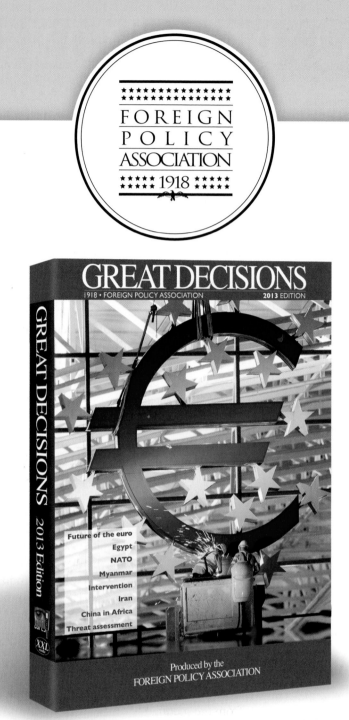

The Foreign Policy Association at 95

THE FOREIGN POLICY ASSOCIATION's mission today—as it has been throughout its 95-year history—is to contribute to a more vibrant democracy through citizen participation in the foreign policy process. A private, nonprofit, nonpartisan educational organization, FPA serves as a catalyst for developing awareness, understanding of and informed opinion on U.S. foreign policy and global issues. It is the nation's oldest organization devoted to citizen education in international affairs.

Harking back to its very beginnings, FPA is inclusive and seeks to engage the public as a whole. "In a democracy," President Franklin D. Roosevelt wrote to Major General Frank R. McCoy, then FPA president, "the Government functions with the consent of the whole people. The latter must be guided by the facts. The Foreign Policy Association is performing a high duty in facilitating the lucid presentation of the facts of world problems and their impact upon the United States."

FPA provides a forum that illuminates the hard choices facing the United States in an increasingly interdependent and multi-polar world. Indeed, FPA continues to be the principal public forum in New York City for foreign policy addresses, attracting broad national and international attention. Over the years, U.S. presidents from FDR to Ronald Reagan and Bill Clinton, have delivered major addresses before FPA audiences. Likewise, in recent years, world leaders from every continent have graced FPA's forum, including the prime ministers of Australia, Greece, Japan, India, Ireland, Italy, South Africa, Spain, Sweden, and Turkey, and the presidents of Chile, Indonesia, Mexico, Mongolia and Senegal, among others.

The diversity of FPA audiences provides an excellent forum for world leaders to communicate directly with a broad cross-section of the American public. All of FPA's events attract informed individuals from the financial, business, and academic communities, as well as from the media.

Among its signal accomplishments, FPA founded a dynamic network of close to one hundred World Affairs Councils across the United States. FPA disseminates its New York-based programming, as well as other multimedia content, throughout this network.

By enriching the foreign policy debate through its balanced publications and programs, FPA occupies a unique space in civil society. For nearly a century, FPA has championed the use of the most powerful communications tools of the day to reach out to the public.

- In the 1920's, FPA used the power of print to syndicate articles in 300 newspapers nationwide.

- In the 1940's, FPA pioneered international affairs radio in partnership with the NBC network.

- In the 1950's, FPA employed billboard ad campaigns to promote its national network of grass-root discussion groups as Americans took to newly built highways.

- In the 1960's, FPA's Great Decisions briefing book took advantage of the explosion in national magazine subscriptions across the country.

Today, www.fpa.org receives a record number of hits as one of the most visited international affairs websites. Despite the rapid growth of the Internet, an effective way to reach the public is through television. Nearly three quarters of Americans receive their information about the world from television. FPA produces and distributes the longest running international affairs television show on the PBS network.

In recent years, FPA has sought to reach young people before the dew of curiosity evaporates. Great Decisions in the Classroom has focused FPA resources on high school teacher education. Great Decisions on Campus has introduced FPA's pedagogical materials in over 1,100 university and college campuses. FPA's upcoming joint venture with Scholastic Inc. will introduce Great Decisions to sixteen million middle school students.

FPA is committed to bringing along future generations of leaders in the public and private sectors, who are well-versed in world affairs. Three distinct initiatives have been launched in pursuit of this goal:

Foreign Policy Association University provides insights to launch successful careers for future diplomats, as well as for other professionals seeking careers in global affairs.

FPA's World Leadership Forum provides a unique parley in which to exchange views about global challenges and to identify creative responses to those challenges. Over 60 heads of government have participated in the Forum. A testimonial from the Head of the Department of Social Sciences at the United States Military Academy at West Point described the Forum as the best academic trip the 30 cadets had experienced during their time at the Academy.

The John C. Whitehead Fellows Program gives 80 young leaders access to all of FPA Fellows' and Board programming.

These initiatives form one of the nation's premier post-graduate programs in international affairs.

FPA's service to the nation is performed with no government support. FPA operates strictly on the basis of private funding. Individuals, corporations and foundations have enabled FPA to fulfill its critical mission.

FPA's role as a source of objective information on world affairs has never been more important. In an increasingly interconnected world, public access to in-depth, contextual information about global issues is vital. By offering Great Decisions, the leading U.S. grass-roots outreach program on world affairs, FPA contributes to expanding citizen engagement in the foreign policy process, as well as to a sustainable foreign policy.

From "basic materials in plain language for weekly study and discussion sessions," Great Decisions has flourished into a multi-dimensional global studies program adapted to multiple formats, including informal discussion groups, public lectures and formal secondary school and university courses. The secret to the longevity of this program? In a word, excellence.

Noel V. Lateef
President and CEO
Foreign Policy Association

Future of the euro
by Erik Jones

Spanish Prime Minister Mariano Rajoy, French President Francois Hollande, Italian Prime Minister Mario Monti and German Chancellor Angela Merkel (L-R) met to achieve a consensus on the handling of Europe's growing financial crisis. (CRISTIANO LARUFFA/PRESIDENZA DEL CONSIGLIO/POOL/GETTY IMAGES)

EUROPEAN SOVEREIGN DEBT MARKETS are in crisis and Europe's political leaders seem unable to forge an effective response. Despite numerous summits and bailout agreements, the number and size of the countries caught up in the turmoil only seems to increase. The crisis in Greece started in April and May of 2010; Ireland called for assistance the following October; Portugal required a bailout in spring 2011; Italy descended into crisis the following autumn, only narrowly avoiding a bailout of its own; by the summer of 2012 Spain was seeking European help for its banking industry and most experts believed a full bailout of the country was all but inevitable.

The stakes are high and continue to mount as problems engulf an ever wider share of the European marketplace: this crisis threatens not only to undermine the European single currency, the euro, but also to send powerful shockwaves through an already enfeebled world economy. The

implications for the United States are acute. U.S. banks and businesses regard the risk of an economic crisis in Europe as the greatest threat to jobs and investment. The transatlantic economic relationship is the most important on the globe in terms of financial flows and cross-border investment. Europe is also a major market for American exports and so a major source of jobs. President Obama's administration clearly recognizes the urgency of the situation. U.S. Treasury Secretary Timo-

ERIK JONES *is Professor and Director of the European Studies Program at the Paul H. Nitze School of Advanced International Studies and Head of Europe at Oxford Analytica. He is also a Senior Research Fellow at Nuffield College, Oxford. He specializes in European political economy and the transatlantic relationship. His most recent publications are* Weary Policeman: American Power in an Age of Austerity *(2012), with Dana Allin, and* The Oxford Handbook on the European Union *(2012), which he edited with Anand Menon and Stephen Weatherill.*

Mario Draghi, president of the European Central Bank, speaks during a news conference.
(HANNELORE FOERSTER/BLOOMBERG/GETTY IMAGES)

thy Geithner has made numerous trips across the Atlantic to urge his European counterparts to take control of events. The chairman of the Federal Reserve, Ben Bernanke, is in constant contact with his European counterpart, European Central Bank (ECB) President Mario Draghi. And President Obama has intervened personally through conversations with German Chancellor Angela Merkel, French President François Hollande and Italian Prime Minister Mario Monti.

Meanwhile, market participants are all too aware of the dangers involved and so are taking steps to safeguard their money. In practice, this means investors are selling their assets in Greece, Ireland, Italy, Spain and Portugal to purchase government bonds in "safe" countries like Germany, Switzerland, Denmark and Norway. The problem is that this flight to safety is making Europe's sovereign debt crisis worse. The Greek government has long had difficulty marshalling control over its accounts. Nevertheless, it was the flow of money out of Greece in the early months of 2010 that made it impossible for the Greek government to meet its financial obligations. The much larger flight to safety from European investors is what threatens Italy and Spain now.

What can be done?

Only a strong and credible response by Europe's policymakers can restore confidence sufficiently to bring the crisis to an end. Unfortunately, that credibility has been damaged by the "muddling through" strategy that European political leaders have chosen to follow. Each time Europe's leaders fail to convince the markets with their proposals to solve the crisis, they make it harder to restore confidence the next time around. They also place strains on shared institutions like the 188-member International Monetary Fund (IMF) and major allies like the U.S. and Japan. The danger is that Europeans will not only lose the faith of the markets, but that they will run out of good will internationally as well. U.S. policymakers must decide whether to continue supporting European efforts or to resort to a more difficult and risky strategy of "tough love."

So far only the ECB and the IMF have demonstrated effective leadership. Time and again the ECB has stepped into the markets to provide a stop-gap measure by offering unlimited loans to the European banking system or by making outright purchases of European sovereign debt in secondary markets. For its part, the IMF has offered its

long experience in reorganizing sovereign debt markets, guiding countries toward more sustainable fiscal policies and coaxing private sector creditors to support distressed government finances. The Federal Reserve also has a role to play in giving the ECB access to liquidity in dollars. However, the actions of these institutions are not enough to solve Europe's problems; at best they can only hold market forces at bay. Only decisive action by Europe's political leadership can bring an end to the crisis. And that decisiveness has so far failed to materialize.

It wasn't meant to end this way

To understand the current situation in Europe it is necessary to go back to the late 1980s, a little more than a decade before the start of Europe's economic and monetary union. The great European project of the day was to complete the integration of national markets for goods and services in order to make Europe more efficient and more competitive. The European economy struggled throughout the 1980's with very high rates of unemployment and low rates of economic growth. By contrast, the U.S. was growing rapidly and Asian economies like Japan and South Korea constituted a powerful threat to European manufacturing.

The European Economic Community (EEC) of 12 West European countries embarked on a project to eliminate all trade barriers by the start of 1993. Much of this effort involved the streamlining of regulatory differences between one country and the next. However, the project soon expanded to include the elimination of capital controls and the creation of a single European financial space, where banks could operate more easily across national borders.

This project had gained momentum with the collapse of communism in Central and Eastern Europe, the rapid unification of Germany and the popularity of European integration. By the start of the 1990's, European integration was more popular than ever in its history, and the possibility of creating a true European Union—rather than just an "economic community"—seemed within reach.

National politicians began to work toward a notion of common European citizenship, looked for ways to promote more democratic input at the European level, and sought to streamline the institutions for collective decisionmaking.

However, the process of eliminating national barriers implied costs as well as benefits. By integrating capital markets, Europe's political leaders knew they would unleash powerful speculative forces as savings and investment moved across national borders. Such speculation threatened to undermine the Continent's fragile system of fixed but adjustable exchange rates. In the worst case scenario, if currencies are whipped about by international capital flows, this could undermine the international trade in goods and services as well. Hence European politicians decided to fix their national exchange rates irrevocably through the creation of a monetary union and the replacement of national currencies with the euro.

The initial proposals for monetary union were made before the fall of the Berlin Wall and the collapse of communism. With the rapid unification of Germany, however, these proposals were folded into the wider package of reforms that created the EU. Moreover, the goals of the two sides of the Treaty on European Union (the so-called "Maastricht Treaty" after the name of the Dutch city where the document was signed in February 1992) were complimentary. Both monetary union and political union would bring stability to the European continent, each in its own way.

Another price to be paid was in terms of economic policy. For the Europeans to share a common currency, they had to accept that the macroeconomic performance of each country was a common interest of them all. This notion of common interest has three implications: governments have to learn to live with the same rate of domestic price inflation, cannot borrow excessively or sustain excessive public debt, and must undertake reforms to streamline and improve the function of labor markets—

not just once, but on a continuing basis as technology changes working patterns and as populations change over time.

Not all of these implications were eagerly embraced by governments across Europe. Some, like the British, opted to stay out of the single currency and refused to accept any restriction on government taxation and spending. Others, like the Danes and the Swedes, accepted the discipline of policy coordination across countries but remained more skeptical about joining the euro. Nevertheless, all European countries— including Britain, Denmark and Swe-

introduce the euro. Indeed, by September 1992, the British government found itself unable to support the value of the pound against the stronger European currencies. The Italians were ejected from the European system of fixed-but-adjustable exchange rates as well. Moreover, the forces of market speculation only increased as popular support for monetary integration diminished, with market actors betting (successfully) that politicians would not raise interest rates enough to stabilize exchange rates. European currency markets were rocked again in 1993 and 1995, lead-

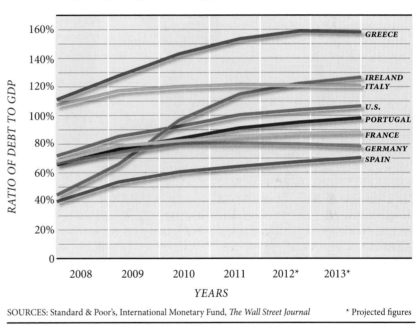

Debt-to-GDP Ratios : 2008–2013*

RATIO OF DEBT TO GDP

GREECE
IRELAND
ITALY
U.S.
PORTUGAL
FRANCE
GERMANY
SPAIN

2008 2009 2010 2011 2012* 2013*

YEARS

SOURCES: Standard & Poor's, International Monetary Fund, *The Wall Street Journal*   * Projected figures

den—accepted the basic principle that their economies are interdependent and that to remain competitive at the global level they would have to work more closely together.

Early stumbles, rapid improvement

The initial steps toward monetary integration were not easy. On the contrary, popular support declined rapidly soon after the signing of the Maastricht Treaty and currency markets went into turmoil. The speculative forces unleashed by capital market integration began to operate long before politicians could

ing many observers to question whether monetary integration would ever come about.

The process proved to be both adaptive and resilient. The newly renamed EU began to accept greater responsibility for economic performance. A 1993 policy paper called for new efforts to promote "jobs, growth, [and] competitiveness" by eliminating excess regulation and streamlining European welfare states.

The European Commission—the executive arm of the EU—also pushed forward legislation to facilitate financial market integration and to help money flow from countries with excess savings to countries sorely in need of capital for investment. Finally Europe's leaders recommitted themselves to the project of monetary integration by negotiating a new pact for stability that would commit governments, including Britain, Denmark and Sweden, to strive to balance their fiscal accounts over the medium-to-long term and to take swift action to correct excessive

deficits. And heavily indebted countries like Belgium, Ireland, and Italy made strong commitments to bring their public finances back into check.

Market participants reacted favorably to the changed environment, and the integration of European capital markets, coupled with the promise of a single European currency, sparked a shift in the pattern of savings and investment across countries. Specifi-

cally, large institutional investors in the richer countries of northern Europe began purchasing sovereign debt obligations—meaning government bonds and treasury certificates—in the poorer countries along the Mediterranean.

The results were dramatic: by the end of the 1990's, long-term interest rates converged across the Continent, meaning that companies in any part of Europe could borrow at much the same cost as companies in any other part. The difference in long-term government borrowing costs between Greece and Germany, for example, collapsed from almost 17 percentage points in 1993 to less than one percent by the year 2000.

This had important effects on government borrowing and productivity growth. Governments in the poorer countries along the Mediterranean found it easier to finance (and so also consolidate) their government borrowing; meanwhile firms in the same countries were able to finance investments in labor-saving technology and so increase the productivity of their manufacturing.

As always, there was a dark cloud as well as a silver lining. Those countries that lent money were also exporting increasing volumes of goods and services relative to what they were importing and those countries that borrowed money wound up importing more than they could export.

The result was an explosion in what economists call macroeconomic imbalances—current account surpluses in one part of Europe being matched by deficits somewhere else—not unlike the relationship between the U.S. and China during the 2000's. Over time, this meant that the poorer countries along the Mediterranean were building up debts to the richer countries of northern Europe that would eventually have to be repaid (just as the U.S. grew increasingly indebted to China).

The point to note, however, is that the European economy was roughly in balance with the outside world; Europeans were developing as a discrete and integrated unit and so taking care of themselves. So long as governments

A sculpture by Belgian artist May Claerhout depicts a woman holding up the symbol of the euro stands outside the European Parliament building in Brussels, Belgium. (EYEVINE/REDUX)

across the EU remained committed to the notion that their national economic performance was a matter of common interest for the EU as a whole, they should have been able to manage their interdependence.

Strong currency, weak politics

Alas, not all EU members are created equal, economically or politically. Some, like Germany, are large and powerful. Others, like Greece or Ireland, are smaller and weaker. The differences are obvious, but they do not sit well with the values underpinning Europe's shared political institutions and economic interdependence. While the EU operates under the fiction that all countries should be bound by the same rules, the reality is much less egalitarian. Some countries have more say than others in setting the rules; the same countries are also more able to break the rules.

The stability pact that was negotiated to ensure sound fiscal policies is a good example. The German government was the major force behind the agreement. In 1993, the German constitutional court decided that the Maastricht Treaty would violate the German basic law (or constitution) if the European monetary union it had to offer was substantially different from the deal German parliamentarians thought they were agreeing to at the time of ratification. Since that deal included a guarantee that the new European currency would deliver absolute price stability, Europe's politicians would have to ensure that absolute price stability was what the new single currency provided, or else some future German government could lose a constitutional challenge and so have to pull out.

The wording here is complicated because the decision pivots on a constitutional provision protecting the sanctity of the relationship between voters and their representatives. The argument is that any unexpected price inflation at the European level would undermine this cornerstone of German democracy. The legal reasoning is not entirely self-evident, but the implications are straightforward. The other European

Activists demonstrate in Frankfurt, Germany, aiming at occupying the central Frankfurt financial district and calling for an end to the imposition of austerity measures on debt-ridden European nations. (HERMANN BREDEHORST/POLARIS)

countries would have to make a pact to ensure the stability of the euro or Germany could not participate. It was only later, in 1997, when a newly elected center-left government in France said it could not agree to any new commitment that did not also take the problem of unemployment into account, that the agreement became known as the stability "and growth" pact. Nevertheless, it was clear from the start that Germany was the most important participant and so the price stability of the euro was paramount. This extended also to the notion that the ECB should be politically independent.

A strong commitment to fiscal discipline in a monetary union that is dedicated to price stability and where exchange rates between countries are irrevocably fixed leaves few policy instruments for governments to tackle the problem of unemployment. This problem became immediately apparent in September 1998 when Germany elected a center-left government of its own.

Facing a persistently high level of unemployment, the new Social Democratic finance minister, Oskar Lafontaine, immediately demanded that the ECB take jobs and growth into consideration in the conduct of monetary policy. Europe's other finance ministers, including the French Socialist Dominique

Strauss-Kahn, were unimpressed. Having just agreed to Germany's demands to embrace a stability pact focusing narrowly on prices, they were not ready to move in the opposite direction.

Lafontaine soon resigned as finance minister and Germany appeared to return to its traditional preference for very low rates of inflation. Nevertheless, the fact that Lafontaine stood up to the politically independent ECB made it clear that the rules for macroeconomic policy coordination were open to question, at least for Germany, and perhaps for other countries as well. Europe's politicians had built a framework for constraining macroeconomic performance within the single currency and yet they were reluctant to enforce it. Hence when the EU's council of economics and finance ministers (Ecofin Council) tried to reprimand the Irish government for failing to tighten fiscal policy in 2001, it was unsurprising that the Irish prime minister (or taoiseach), Bertie Ahern, chose to ignore his colleagues rather than embrace his commitment to Europe.

The decision by the Ecofin Council not to challenge Portugal or Germany for running excessive fiscal deficits in February 2002 was even less impressive. Rather than risk a confrontation with Germany, the European institutions chose to accept the government's

1

assurances that it could keep its finances in check. Germany's deficit only continued to grow over the next year and both France and Italy had problems as well.

The European institutions could no longer avoid taking action, but the powerful countries did not want to accept discipline. The decisions by the French and German governments to circumvent the procedures for fiscal policy coordination in November 2003 showed clearly that the rules need not apply.

The moral hazard

Europe's political weakness was only part of the problem for the monetary union. The moral hazard created by rapidly declining interest rates ultimately proved more important. This notion of moral hazard means, in essence, that market actors face opportunities that they would be better off not taking and yet they take them because they figure they can somehow escape the consequences. This is what happens when interest rates fall suddenly in economies that are used to paying a lot to borrow money. Suddenly, investors that have long been priced out of the market can afford to borrow and investment opportunities that have never been tested seem to make sense.

The problem is made worse when the reason interest rates are falling is a

sudden inflow of capital from abroad. The foreign investors providing the capital have little patience to learn about the assets they are acquiring and the domestic banks that are acting as intermediaries have little expertise in managing rapidly expanding asset portfolios or distinguishing between good borrowers and bad. Here again there are close parallels between what happened in southern Europe and the recent experience of the U.S. during the 2000s.

The moral hazard played out differently from one country to the next. In Ireland, the effects could be seen both in the rapid growth of domestic banks and the commercial real estate market. The Anglo-Irish Bank is a good example. Sean Fitzpatrick, the bank's chairman and chief executive, made his reputation as a banker by making loan decisions quickly.

He did not offer the lowest interest rates on the Irish market, but he could get developers the money they needed faster than the competition. He justified this strategy by pointing out that every sector of the economy interacts with commercial real estate clients through the rental and purchase markets; hence, he believed his asset portfolio of loans against commercial real estate developments was perfectly diversified.

Similar reasoning could be made with respect to real estate development

in Spain, consumer credit in Portugal or sovereign debt in Greece. In each case, foreign investors believed they were insulated from the risk of default because their assets somehow touched upon or represented the whole of society.

What the inflow of credit actually created, however, was a massive asset price bubble. Irish commercial real estate prices grew far beyond reasonable values even as overlapping real estate development projects undermined each others' business models. Spain built more housing and commercial real estate than could ever find domestic demand. Portugal saw consumption grow into unsustainable levels of household debt. And Greece found it all too easy to finance excessive (and unaccounted for) levels of government borrowing.

In each case, foreign investors were blissfully unaware. Instead large investment firms channeled ever more savings from countries like Germany into the periphery of the euro zone from one year to the next. Not all of that money was wasted. Productivity growth in Greece raced ahead of productivity growth in Germany during the 2000s where it had trailed slightly in the 1990s.

It is not true that the peripheral countries were uncompetitive either. On the contrary, manufacturing employment increased in Portugal, Ireland, Italy, Greece and Spain during the 2000s while it declined in Germany. Both world and intra-European export market shares held up better in the more peripheral countries than in Britain or Scandinavia.

Nevertheless, enough of the money lent by wealthy countries like Germany to the Mediterranean countries went into asset bubbles or worthless investments so that it would be impossible for the poorer countries to honor their obligations if their northern European creditors would suddenly call those loans home.

Hence the stability of the monetary union rested on the faith that northern European investors would never have a reason to do that. That faith proved unfounded. ∎

Doctors and health workers hold banners in Barcelona, Spain, during a 2011 protest on planned cuts due to government debt. (MANU FERNANDEZ/AP/CORBIS)

The trouble with banks

THE PROBLEM started in 2007 with the crisis in U.S. housing markets and structured financial products like mortgage-backed securities and collateralized debt obligations. This was the beginning of the economic and financial crisis that has dragged on for five years and more. Initially, the European single currency weathered the crisis well; European banks did not. The casualties were not limited to banks within the single currency. British banks, Hungarian banks, Icelandic banks and Swedish banks were also badly affected. The reason was that no one knew which banks were most exposed to U.S. mortgages and so banks stopped lending to one another. For some banks, like the British mortgage-lender Northern Rock, this freezing up of the interbank lending market proved catastrophic. Northern Rock relied on loans from other banks to finance its mortgages. When those loans dried up, it had to turn to the Bank of England for support. In turn, the Bank of England made it known in the markets that the Northern Rock required emergency liquidity. This sparked a run on the bank as depositors lined up to get their savings back. The British government ended up nationalizing Northern Rock.

The situation in Europe worsened each time some new problem emerged in the U.S. The rescue of investment bank Bear Stearns in March 2008 sparked another tightening in European interbank lending markets; so did the bailout of mortgage giants Fannie Mae and Freddie Mac the following summer. However, it was the collapse of Lehman Brothers on Sept. 15, 2008, that sent the European markets into a rout. Iceland effectively declared bankruptcy soon thereafter; Hungary went to the IMF for a bailout; and the Baltic states, particularly Latvia, looked set to abandon their fixed exchange rates with the euro.

The situation in Ireland was particularly dramatic. The Irish economy had grown from one of the poorer countries of Europe to one of the wealthiest over

Northern Rock shareholders protest outside one of the bank's branches in London in 2009.
(SIMON DAWSON/BLOOMBERG/GETTY IMAGES)

the previous two decades and the Irish banks had grown even more impressively. By 2007, they held assets worth three times the national economy; taken together with foreign banks domiciled in Ireland, the ratio of banking assets to gross domestic product (GDP) was much higher. Without access to international bank lending, the Irish banks simply did not have enough domestic deposits to remain liquid, and, faced with mounting losses on assets held in the U.S., it was an open question whether they could remain solvent. Under Taoiseach Brian Cowen, the Irish government decided to fill in the gap, first by announcing that Irish deposits would be covered by national insurance and then by pledging to underwrite all of the liabilities of the Irish banking system with the resources of the Irish state. Cowen's goal was to restore confidence to the domestic banking system in order to restart inter-bank lending. In doing so, however, he hugely expanded the public debt to pay for bank bailouts. Ireland's public debt-to-GDP ratio was just under 25 percent; by 2011 it was more than 100 percent and still rising.

The problem was not limited to Ireland or even to banks on the periphery. The banks in the wealthier countries at the core of the euro area were exposed to the crisis as well. Hence, Belgian and Dutch banks also ran into difficulties; so did banks in Germany. These were all countries that exported capital, lending money both to other parts of the euro area and to finance investments in the U.S. Since this money was originally financed by domestic savings in these countries greater than domestic levels of investment, it is worth explaining why they could not simply absorb the losses on their investments and walk away.

The answer has to do with leverage. The Belgian, Dutch and German banks used their domestic deposits to borrow even more money abroad. This way they had the resources to double- and triple-down on their investments. The problem is that the losses they experienced in the U.S. and elsewhere quickly threatened to wipe out that original domestic capital.

The results of this excessive leverage in the banking system of the wealthier

European countries can be seen in the rapid demise of French-Belgian Dexia and Belgian-Dutch Fortis, two banking and insurance conglomerates with significant operations in France (Dexia) and the Netherlands (Fortis), among other places. Within a matter of days after the bankruptcy of Lehman Brothers, the Belgian government found itself in an intractable situation. It did not have the resources to bail out both Dexia and Fortis, it was unwilling to take the same gamble made by Cowen in Ireland and it could not count on the patience of the French or Dutch governments.

The Dutch government moved to separate that part of Fortis most active in the Netherlands, leaving the Belgians to sort out the rest; the French government agreed to bail out Dexia in a more cooperative arrangement. Both Dexia and Fortis were effectively bailed out as a consequence. The Hypo Real Estate holding in Germany suffered much the same fate.

Ironically, the banks in the poorer Mediterranean countries were less exposed to U.S. losses because their businesses either were more narrowly focused on domestic assets or were managed more conservatively. The large Spanish banks, for example, set aside additional capital buffers against potential losses and the large Italian banks only rarely looked to make investments abroad (UniCredit being an exception to the rule).

Nevertheless, these Mediterranean banks were exposed to the second- and third-order consequences of the crisis. They relied on the wealthier northern European banks for new inflows of capital and they depended upon having a healthy domestic economy to keep their borrowers in business.

These secondary and tertiary effects grew in importance over time and as the initial shock of the financial crisis mutated into a deep and lasting economic recession. This is where the losses incurred in Spanish commercial real estate markets became important through their impact on the balance sheets of the small regional savings banks (or *cajas*).

As the crisis wore on, more and more developers declared bankruptcy and defaulted on their debts. In turn, this shut down construction projects and raised unemployment, further deepening the recession. For its part, the Spanish government sought to stabilize the cajas and prop up the domestic economy. Doing so, however, meant running the government ever deeper into debt. The situation was not as dramatic as in Ireland but it was painful nonetheless. The ratio of Spanish public debt to GDP was just over 36 percent in 2007; by 2011 it was over 68 percent and rising fast. ∎

Blame it on the Greeks

WITHIN THE CONTEXT of Europe's banking crisis, the Greek case was exceptional because it dealt with government borrowing, which, from the start of the single currency, was known to be a problem. Unfortunately, the Greek story is widely misinterpreted. Many economists believe the issue here revolves around an irresponsible government and an uncompetitive economy. If only things were that simple; then, Europe could isolate Greece and end the nightmare.

Unfortunately, the situation shows something altogether more complicated and more dangerous because it reveals how it is the flight to safety by international investors that lies at the heart of the dilemma. All the money that flowed through Europe's integrated capital markets to provide investment on the periphery of the European economy is now being called back home to countries like Germany, Belgium and the Netherlands. Part of the reason is that the northern Europeans need the money back to shore up their domestic banking industry and part is that they no longer have much confidence in the investments they made on the periphery. Either way, it has not only put pressure on the cost of government borrowing on the periphery of the euro area, but also drawn much-needed resources from the Mediterranean banks.

This is a complicated story that can be told in either of two ways. One way is to look at the various indicators for competitiveness, employment and export market shares. Greece lost more relative cost advantage (measured in terms of relative real effective exchange rates) before it entered the euro than it lost after joining the single currency; once it joined the euro, Greek manufacturing gained both in terms of productivity and in terms of employment, at least up through 2007; and Greece managed to hold onto as much of its world export market share during the same period as Germany. None of these developments makes sense if Greece's problem is international "competitiveness." But that does not stop the accusations. The unfortunate reality in economics is that there is no objective measure of competitiveness and the data do not paint a consistent picture. As a result, most analysts stop as soon as they find evidence to confirm their preferred interpretation. That explains why it has been so easy for politicians to misinterpret the underlying dynamics.

The other way to tell the story is to focus on three overlapping chronologies—for policy pronouncements, capital flows and interest rate movements. This overlapping narrative points to a simple conclusion. Market participants always suspected that the Greek government borrowed recklessly and they were unsurprised when the problem turned out to be larger than they expected. What did surprise them was that Europe's leaders were unwilling to do anything to address the problem. What made matters worse was the sudden realization that European leaders were going to make the private sector bear all the losses.

This overlapping narrative starts soon after the collapse of Lehman Brothers in 2008. The Greek government announced a slight upward revision in its deficit projections and the market reaction was disproportionate. Money flowed quickly out of the country and Greek interest rates rose suddenly against Germany. Indeed, by early 2009, markets were charging the Greek government more to borrow over 10 years than they were charging the Irish government. Given that the taoiseach had just pledged to underwrite the liabilities of the entire Irish banking system, the relatively higher cost of Greek borrowing was significant. Standard & Poor's, the ratings agency, further fueled the fires by downgrading the Greek government's creditworthiness, citing the poor quality of Greek fiscal data as part of its explanation.

The German finance minister, a Social Democrat named Peer Steinbrück, recognized the problem of capital flight from Greece and attempted to calm the situation. Speaking to a business audience in Germany, he pledged that no government participating in the euro would be allowed to go bankrupt. He later sent his assistant to offer the same assurances to the *Financial Times*. The markets responded accordingly. Money stopped flowing out of Greece and started slowly to trickle back in again. By the late spring of 2009, Greek borrowing costs moved below those of Ireland and the sense of crisis abated. Greek fiscal accounting did not improve. Indeed, the IMF complained publicly about the poor quality of Greek fiscal data during its annual consultations with the Greek government. Nevertheless, market participants were reassured that the Greek government would be able to meet its financial obligations.

In October 2009, the Greek government announced another, much larger upward revision in its fiscal deficit. This time the announcement followed an EU mission to improve the quality of Greek fiscal accounting. It also followed a popular election that saw a change in Greece's government. However, the market response was very different from the previous year. Interest rates on long-term government borrowing remained stable; money actually flowed into Greece rather than fleeing to safety elsewhere. By implication, investors

Civil service workers protest austerity measures in the streets of Athens as unemployment has risen to 20 percent in Greece. Drastic reforms of the public sector are a controversial part of the country's strategy to improve its financial situation. (MARO KOURI/POLARIS)

were not alarmed by the latest revision in the data. They only started to pull their money out of Greece in significant amounts about four to five months later.

The difference between 2009 and 2010 was not the solvency of the Greeks but the attitude of the German government. The Christian Democrats used the 2009 parliamentary elections as an opportunity to end their grand coalition with the Social Democrats and to start a

new, center-right coalition with the liberal Free Democratic Party. As a result, the finance ministry was suddenly unwilling to bail out other European countries and the chancellor, the Christian Democrat Angela Merkel, insisted that those governments that get into trouble should take responsibility. This new, tougher line was popular domestically. It hewed closely to the formal rules for the economic and monetary union as

Greece faces a severe economic crisis as debt has soared. The effects have rippled from the Athens Stock Exchange through the rest of Europe. (YANNIS KONTOS/POLARIS)

Greeks did have poor fiscal accounting. They also have a bloated public sector, poor tax collection and a host of other problems. But they have had those problems for a long time and have made some improvements (albeit very slowly). In any case investors were well aware of these deficiencies. The shortcomings of the Greeks were not why the markets reacted; the lack of European solidarity was. Unfortunately, by blaming the Greek crisis on the Greeks, Europe's political leaders gave themselves an excuse to muddle through rather than responding decisively; why should they put their good money at risk to bail out a people who are so manifestly undeserving?

Europe's political leaders also ensured that the sovereign debt crisis would spread across the periphery of the euro area. When Chancellor Merkel and then-French President Nicolas Sarkozy made it known in October 2010 that they would seek to impose losses on private-sector holdings of Greek government bonds, investors started to worry about what this implied about the situation with respect to Ireland. Money flowed out of Ireland, borrowing costs rose and the Irish government had to request a bailout. A similar pattern followed in Portugal in the late spring of 2011, when it became clear that private sector losses in Greece would have to be larger as part of a second bailout package.

The discussion of private sector losses in the second Greek bailout was what also dragged Italy into the sovereign debt crisis. The Italian government has a lot of public debt but it also has relatively strong fiscal institutions and a healthy balance between taxation and spending. Moreover, most of the debt could be financed with domestic savings. Italy's economic relationship with the outside world is close to balanced, and so the Italian economy does not rely on foreign savings to finance domestic investment. Nevertheless, Italian government debt securities have been attractive to foreigners because they pay a relatively high rate of interest. As a result, while Italy could finance its debt using domestic resources, it does not do

well. Nevertheless, it created concern among investors that their holdings of Greek bonds were no longer safe.

When Merkel insisted that any bailout would come as a last resort, after Greece no longer had access to private capital markets, and with the participation of the IMF, the markets panicked. Money surged out of Greece and long-term government borrowing costs skyrocketed. Just two weeks after Merkel made her position clear at the

March 2010 European Council summit, the Greek government admitted that it would have to seek international assistance. By early May, the EU and the IMF worked out the details of a bailout. And a week later, the EU announced new arrangements that could be extended to other countries that got into trouble.

By blaming it on the Greeks, Europe's leaders fundamentally misunderstood the nature of the threat. The

so in practice because foreigners have been willing to pay more (and so earn less) than Italians to hold Italian debt.

Unfortunately, those same foreigners suddenly started to worry about their potential losses in Italy's €1.8 trillion debt market. Starting in July 2011, they began to slow down their purchases or even sell out their holdings of Italian government debt. They also began to pay closer attention to the strange world of Italian politics. The result was a near disaster for Italian public finances that was only narrowly averted once the prime minister resigned from office and the country's largest political parties agreed to support an unelected government of experts. The "technocratic" government headed by Mario Monti came to power in December 2011 with roughly 15 months to reform the economy before the next scheduled round of parliamentary elections. It is an almost impossible challenge made all the worse by the problems elsewhere on the euro area periphery, and particularly in Spain.

Doom loop

The Italian case revealed a particular form of contagion that causes the crisis to spread from one country to the next by attacking either sovereign debt markets or major banks. Economists call this the "doom loop." The comparison between Italy and Spain shows how the mechanism works. In the Italian case, international investors were worried about their losses on investments in Italian sovereign debt. But they also knew that the institutions most exposed to losses on Italian sovereign debt were the Italian banks. So once Italian bonds ran into trouble because international investors started withdrawing from the markets, it made sense to start selling the stock of the Italian banking sector as well. And once the banks stocks started falling in the markets, it made little sense for banks from other countries to lend money to Italian banks; and so Italy's access to international banking markets dried up.

The situation in Spain was the reverse. The government started out with a low level of public debt and the larger private banks were secure. Nevertheless, the cajas showed consistent signs of weakness and so required government bailouts. As the Spanish government put more money into the cajas, however, the stability of its public finances started to look worse.

Hence international investors started to move their money out of Spanish government bonds, imposing losses on the banking system—both the cajas and the relatively more stable large private institutions—where the holdings of Spanish sovereign debt are most concentrated. In this context, it started to make sense for international investors to start selling their holdings of Spanish banking stocks and for international banks to limit their lending to Spain. As in Italy, the end result was the same. Both the Spanish government and the Spanish banking system suffered from the flight of foreign capital.

This same dynamic is operating across the peripheral countries of the euro area. As a result, most of the banks in these countries find themselves cut off from access to liquidity from the outside world. Where the dream of integration had been to create a common market, the crisis is prompting a renationalization of European finance. Indeed, the only institution holding the European financial economy together is the ECB, which is providing unprecedented access to day-to-day liquidity (or money) in order to support the banking systems of countries like Greece, Ireland, Portugal, Italy and Spain.

Worse, this money has to come from somewhere, and that is the central banks of the northern European countries like Germany. Perversely, these northern European central banks are loaning money to the central banks on the periphery of the euro area so that those central banks can hand it over to domestic banks in the Mediterranean countries, which have to give the money back to depositors, who then take the money to open up accounts in Germany.

The situation in Greece has become particularly untenable. The politicians have been unable to make progress in fiscal consolidation given the weakness of the economy; the electorate threatens to run out of patience by voting for anti-austerity political parties; the IMF cannot make payments for the bailout until the Greek government has met certain conditions; the northern European countries seem unwilling to pick up the slack or to continue with the bailout program in case the IMF has to withdraw; and the ECB has made it clear that it cannot provide indefinite liquidity sup-

A large housing construction project sits unfinished in Burgos, Spain in 2011. The financial crisis has frozen many development projects across the country. (BERT SPIERTZ/HOLLANDSE HOOGTE/REDUX)

port for the Greek banks. The Greeks are beginning to prepare for the worst and are moving even more money out of the country to protect themselves.

Political leaders have slowly awakened to this dilemma but they have painted themselves too tightly into a corner to forge an effective response. Having laid all the blame on the undeserving peoples of the periphery, the political leaders of core countries like Germany, Finland and the Netherlands can no longer find popular support for a comprehensive solution. Market participants are all too aware of this dynamic and they are moving their money to safety accordingly, exacerbating the problem in the process. This raises the real prospect of a European calamity.

ECB President Draghi made a last-ditch effort to restore calm to the market in a speech he delivered to the financial community in London on July 26, 2012. There he warned against the danger of financial disintegration and pledged to do whatever necessary to safeguard the euro. He also made it clear that he expected Europe's politicians to live up to their responsibilities. The question is whether there is still time to do so.

Brass ring

There is a solution, but it is a long shot. To begin with, Europeans need to ask themselves what is the big difference between Europe and the U.S. This comparison is not ideal because the state governments in the U.S. are very different from the national governments in Europe. Nevertheless, the Europeans themselves are fond of using the U.S. experience as a point of reference because it is the only roughly comparable monetary area they know (even if it is also, unlike the euro area, a federal union). The answer has four parts: First, the U.S. has common instruments to share the costs of bailing out banks: Federal Deposit Insurance Company (FDIC) and bank resolution mechanisms. Second, it has common banking oversight as well. These two features are well known. That is why there is so much talk in Europe about the importance of creating a banking

union—which is what the Europeans agreed to do at the June 29, 2012, EU summit. If the Europeans want integrated capital markets, a banking union makes sense. But there is more to the U.S. experience than that.

The third difference between Europe and the U.S. is how U.S. investors move their money to safety. They sell equities and buy bonds, moving up the quality ladder until they end up holding U.S. Treasury instruments. European investors not only move across asset classes, but they also move their money geographically—from Greece, Italy, and Spain, to countries like Germany, the Netherlands and France. This geographic flight to safety has to end, which means that the Europeans need a "risk-free" asset that can circulate everywhere in Europe with the same ease that U.S. Treasury instruments circulate everywhere in the U.S. This is why European politicians need to look again at proposals to create a common Eurobond. They are reluctant to do so because northern Europeans fear that such an instrument would make it too easy for the Mediterranean countries to borrow money and so only make matters worse rather than better. There is some truth that Eurobonds create a danger of moral hazard, but it is clear that Europe is already suffering from that under present conditions and there are ways to structure Eurobonds to make them work better.

The fourth difference is where the contrast between an EU of sovereign member states and a federal U.S. becomes important. The American political system makes it more difficult for different parts of the country to ignore their interdependence with all the rest. Although there is much talk in the U.S. about polarization between Democrats and Republicans, North and South, or the bicoastal regions and the fly-over states, the differences are much less important than the cross-country differences in Europe and the level of solidarity across the U.S. is greater than it is across the EU or the euro area. The Europeans need to learn the importance of that political commitment. It is controversial and yet also essential. If they

continue to blame one another for their economic problems, the situation is unlikely to get better.

Policy questions to consider

The situation in Europe is not going to improve overnight and the implications of a breakdown in the European economy or a collapse of the euro area have never been greater. This raises important questions for U.S. policymakers. Some of these questions are fundamental and relate to the lessons that policymakers should learn from the crisis. Some of the questions are much more practical and concern what any U.S. administration should try to do.

To what extent does the European sovereign debt crisis reveal the failings of the European welfare state model and to what extent does it reveal the breakdown of European integration? The answer here is counterintuitive from an American perspective because the most generous welfare states in Europe are also the wealthiest. Germany offers more public services than Greece, for example. Outside the euro area, Sweden and Denmark offer more public services than Germany. Hence while it is tempting to believe that Europe's problems are the result of the public sector run amok, it is more likely to be a simpler problem of borrowing excessively both in the public sector (as in Greece) and, more frequently, in the private sector (as in everywhere else). Excessive private sector indebtedness is a problem in the U.S. as well.

How much can the U.S. insulate itself from the consequences of Europe's sovereign debt crisis and to what extent should the U.S. government agree to work with European allies to find a solution? The challenge here is to reverse decades of financial globalization and cross-border investment. The U.S. and European economies have grown together tightly since the end of World War II. And that was the objective. Hence the only choice for American policymakers is to work with their European counterparts. This is not an easy

1

option. The Europeans are no more eager to get lessons in economics from the U.S. than Americans are to learn about the virtues of the European "social model."

Should U.S. banking regulators discourage American banks and money market funds from investing in Europe (to limit exposure to potential losses on European investments)?

This is a bit technical but the principle at stake is the same as in the previous question. Financial markets work most efficiently when they channel savings to places where it is most useful for investment. If all that money stays in the U.S., where will it go? This is the liquidity glut problem that Federal Reserve Chairman Bernanke has emphasized as a leading cause of the U.S. financial crisis. If American banks and money market funds hold money back from Europe to invest in subprime mortgages or some new and equally risky instrument, no one will be better off.

Should American banking regulators subject European banks to closer scrutiny when they operate in the U.S.?

This consideration is more straightforward. The European banks actually suffered a lot from the U.S. financial crisis and U.S. regulators have an interest in making sure that does not happen again. Dexia and Fortis are prime examples, but the list of failing banks is long and stretches across the wealthiest countries on the European Continent.

Should the U.S. government encourage its European allies to hold together the single European currency or should it encourage failing countries like Greece to leave the euro?

If Greece were to leave the euro, the consequences would be difficult to predict and the risks are mostly on the downside. That is why Chancellor Merkel is so reluctant to go down that route, even if she does not appreciate having to bail out the Greeks. This is where the story about contagion is important. If Greece were to leave the euro, it would create fear about Ireland, Portugal, Spain and Italy as well. Such fear would only intensify the crisis and

make a collapse of the euro more likely. The consequences for U.S. growth and employment would be immediate and painful.

Should the IMF use its resources – including U.S. capital subscriptions – to bail out rich European countries, or should IMF assistance be limited to technical advice and guidance?

The IMF has a legitimacy problem among emerging market economies and only limited resources to act worldwide. The legitimacy problem stems from the fact that the European countries are overrepresented. Thanks to Greece, they are now calling upon a disproportionate share of IMF resources.

This is a toxic combination viewed from the emerging economies. It is also unnecessary. The IMF could provide technical advice and guidance while insisting that the Europeans pay for themselves—at least within the euro area, but probably also elsewhere. The IMF might choose to use this as leverage to get the Europeans to accept necessary institutional reforms.

Should the Federal Reserve provide access to liquidity in dollars for European banks operating in the U.S. and for European central banks operating in Europe?

This is another technical question that goes to the heart of the dollar as

the world's most important currency. Right now banks in Europe use dollars for much of their day-to-day operations with large multinationals. This means they have both liabilities and assets denominated in dollars that need to be managed. Having the Fed provide dollar-denominated liquidity to the ECB is necessary to make sure these banks remain solvent. By taking away that assistance, the Fed would make European banks more likely to default, which would not be in anyone's best interests.

Should the U.S. withdraw from global capital markets or work more closely with allies in Europe and elsewhere to draft new rules and regulations to make global capital markets more stable?

The interdependence between Europe and the U.S. is now obvious. Hence the interest in having common rules to promote stability in the financial sector is obvious as well. Any differences in the regulations across the Atlantic only make it easier for banks and other financial institutions to try to "game the system" in order to make profits. That is how the European banks became so exposed to risky U.S. financial products in the first place. ∎

✔ **Opinion Ballots** after page 32

discussion questions

1. Consider the history of European economic integration and the common currency. What factors weakened the monetary union? Was the euro crisis inevitable? What parts have been played by individual countries of the EU, such as Germany and France? Does the sovereign debt crisis demonstrate failures in the European welfare state model? What does it reveal about intracontinental dynamics?

2. To what extent can the U.S. insulate itself from the consequences of Europe's sovereign debt crisis and to what extent should the U.S. government agree to work with European allies to find a solution? Should the U.S. attempt to isolate the European crisis, e.g. if U.S. banking regulators discourage American banks and money market funds from investing in Europe (and so exposing themselves to potential losses on European investments)?

3. Should the U.S. withdraw from global capital markets or work more closely with allies in Europe and elsewhere to draft new rules and regulations to make global capital markets more stable?

4. Is more banking regulation the answer? Should an international organization have greater oversight over financial institutions? Should U.S. banking regulators subject European banks to closer scrutiny when they operate in the U.S.? What kind of regulations, if any, could prevent the "moral hazard" described by the author?

5. What would be the implications of a "Grexit" (Greek exit from the euro)? Should the U.S. government encourage its European allies to hold together the single European currency or should it encourage failing countries like Greece to leave the euro?

6. Should the IMF use its resources, including U.S. capital subscriptions, to bail out European countries, or should IMF assistance be limited to technical advice and guidance? Consider the IMF's policies of extending loans and debt forgiveness to countries plagued by economic problems. What kind of options are available for ailing European economies?

suggested readings

Akerlof, George A., and Robert J. Shiller, **Animal Spirits: How Human Psychology Drives the Economy and Why It Matters for Global Capitalism.** Princeton, Princeton University Press, 2009. 256 pp. $16.95 (paper). This book explains the psychological mechanisms underlying the current economic and financial crisis. It is particularly useful for understanding asset market bubbles.

Allin, Dana, and Erik Jones, **Weary Policeman: American Power in an Age of Austerity.** London, Routledge, 2012. 227 pp. $26.95 (paper). This book shows how the economic and financial crisis has changed the conduct of U.S. foreign policy. It also highlights the implications of the European sovereign debt crisis for the U.S.

Hodson, Dermot, **Governing the Euro Area in Good Times and Bad. New York**, Oxford University Press, 2011. 224 pp. $85.00 (hardcover). This is an overview of the political institutions that manage the single European currency. It explains both how they were meant to work and why they broke down.

Jones, Erik, "Italy's Sovereign Debt Crisis." **Survival** 54 (2012). 83–110. This essay explains how Italy got caught up in the European sovereign debt crisis during the period from July to December 2011. Since Italy is the world's third largest sovereign debt market, the threat of an Italian crisis has global implications.

Kindleberger, Charles P., and Robert Z. Aliber, **Manias, Panics and Crashes: A History of Financial Crises**, 6th ed. New York, Palgrave Macmillan, 2011. 368 pp. $20.00 (paper). Kindleberger's classic work is updated by Aliber to cover the collapse of Lehman Brothers and the current crisis. It reveals not only why financial crises occur but also why policy responses are often ineffective.

Lewis, Michael, **Boomerang: Travels in the New Third World**. New York, W.W. Norton & Company, 2011. 240 pp. $16.95 (paper). This book offers a humorous but insightful look at the impact of the economic and financial crisis in countries across Europe.

Lyons, Tom, and Brian Carey, **The Fitzpatrick Tapes: The Rise and Fall of One Man, One Bank, and One Country.** Dublin, Penguin Press, 2011. 304 pp. $11.09 (e-book). Two investigative journalists chart the evolution of the financial crisis in Ireland. They show not only how the Celtic tiger got into trouble but also how politicians made matters worse.

Wolf, Martin, **Fixing Global Finance: How to Curb Financial Crises in the 21st Century.** Baltimore, Johns Hopkins University Press, 2010. 272 pp. $20.95 (paper). This book shows the connection between cross-border capital flows and bad lending practices.

For up-to-date news and analysis of this time-sensitive topic, we recommend the following Internet resources:

EUObserver, <www.euobserver.com>. This site provides a free summary of European press on issues related to the European Union.

Project Syndicate, <http://www.project-syndicate.org>. This is an online forum for commentary on politics, economics, and international affairs that often includes very thoughtful essays on Europe. Most of the commentators are professional academics, but the level of analysis is broadly accessible.

TO LEARN MORE ABOUT THIS TOPIC AND TO ACCESS WEB LINKS TO RESOURCES GO TO www.greatdecisions.org

Egypt: navigating an uncertain transition
by Bruce K. Rutherford

Supporters of the Muslim Brotherhood's presidential candidate, Mohamed Morsi, celebrate his victory with a spectacular fireworks display in Cairo on June 24, 2012. (XINHUA/EYEVINE/REDUX)

THE MIDDLE EAST has experienced extraordinary changes since the beginning of the "Arab Spring" in January 2011—from meaningful progress toward democracy in Tunisia, to gradual reform in Morocco, to civil war in Syria. However, the path of change in Egypt is likely to be of particular importance. Egypt has the Arab world's largest population (83 million in 2011) and largest military, as well as its third-largest economy. It is a prolific source of art, film and literature for the region, and is an important center for Sunni Islamic thought and tradition. Accordingly, political developments in Egypt are likely to serve as a model—or a warning—throughout the region.

The end of Pharaoh

Hosni Mubarak seemed to be the model autocrat. Since assuming power in 1981, he used co-optation and coercion with equal skill to build a wide circle of supporters and to keep opponents at bay. However, the foundations of his rule had been eroding for decades. His regime had its roots in

the revolutionary era of Gamal Abdel Nasser, who came to power in 1952. Nasser and his successors made a commitment to provide citizens with a wide range of services, including jobs in the public sector and the civil service as well as substantial subsidies for food, electricity, gasoline, public transportation, education and medical care. The regime's legitimacy was grounded in providing these benefits. However, the economy simply did not generate sufficient wealth or state revenue to sustain these services, particularly as Egypt's population grew dramatically in the 1980's and 1990's. Mubarak began cutbacks in 1991 as part of a broader market-oriented reform plan. He and his international supporters hoped that a restructuring of the economy to focus on market forces would generate economic growth and satisfy the public's expectations of the government. However, these

BRUCE K. RUTHERFORD *is associate professor of political science at Colgate University. He is the author of* Egypt After Mubarak: Liberalism, Islam, and Democracy in the Arab World *(Princeton University Press, 2008).*

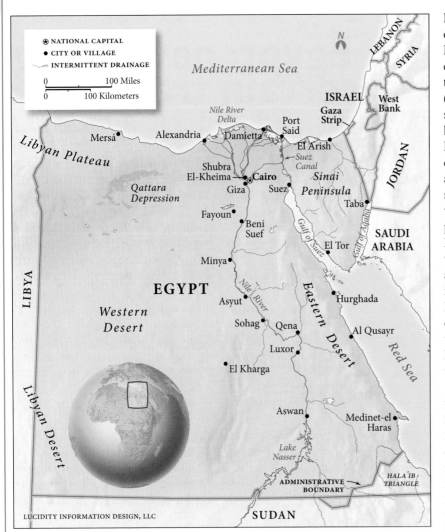

NATIONAL CAPITAL
CITY OR VILLAGE
INTERMITTENT DRAINAGE

0 — 100 Miles
0 — 100 Kilometers

LUCIDITY INFORMATION DESIGN, LLC

November 2010 for the lower house of Parliament, the People's Assembly. Mubarak and his advisers rigged the elections to yield a lopsided victory for the ruling National Democratic Party (NDP), which won 93 percent of the seats. The Muslim Brotherhood, which had led the opposition in the previous Parliament with 88 seats, did not receive any representation. The regime also embarked on a new round of measures to restrict the opposition press, which included closing some newspapers and prosecuting critical journalists. In addition, it reined in the reformist wing of the judiciary, which had been an important voice for electoral honesty in the 2005 elections. Thus, as the public was pushed ever closer to economic desperation, the peaceful avenues for venting its anger—whether through Parliament, the press or the judiciary—were largely closed off.

These pressures came to a head in the protests that began on January 25, 2011. These demonstrations, the largest in Egyptian history, were due, in part, to events in Tunisia. Eleven days earlier, massive crowds in the capital city of Tunis had driven Zine al-Abdine Ben Ali into exile and had shown the capacity of public outrage to effect change. Other factors also contributed to the size of the crowds in Cairo and other Egyptian cities, including online communities that created surprisingly strong bonds among young people that led many to demonstrate for the first time; satellite television (particularly Al Jazeera) whose broadcasts enabled Egyptians to see both the size of the crowds and the regime's brutal response; and the organizational skill of the youth movement, which developed novel ways to outmaneuver Egypt's vast and plodding security apparatus.

Of course, all these efforts would have been for naught if the military had intervened to disperse the demonstrators. The military leadership's decisions not to fire on the protesters and to facilitate Mubarak's departure proved pivotal. Although the complete story behind these decisions is still unknown, it is likely that the generals' thinking was shaped, in part, by concerns over

reforms were implemented imperfectly. The rate of job creation was inadequate and the gains from economic restructuring flowed mostly to a small elite. The privatization plan at the heart of the reform program was plagued by corruption in which state assets were sold at fire-sale prices to businessmen with close ties to the regime. In addition, the country suffered from high rates of inflation that steadily ate away at citizens' purchasing power and pushed many into poverty. At the time of the January 2011 uprising, more than 40 percent of the population fell below the poverty line. In 2008, unemployment among university graduates had already reached 25 percent, according to the United Nations Development

This article uses material from the paperback edition of the author's book, Egypt after Mubarak: Liberalism, Islam, and Democracy in the Arab World.

Programme. As the legitimacy of the regime steadily declined and the economic situation for many citizens continued to deteriorate, Egyptians had few peaceful ways to express their anger. Opposition parties were small and ineffectual, while civil society groups were carefully monitored and regulated by the state.

In 2010, several developments intensified the economic and political pressures that led to the uprising. Inflation had been a constant bane in the lives of many Egyptians, averaging more than 10 percent for much of the decade preceding the uprising. This problem worsened sharply, with food prices rising 37 percent in the two years prior to the uprising. As many citizens' economic situation worsened, the political institutions that ostensibly represented them became even less responsive. This was particularly true during the elections in

ARCTIC OCEAN

Queen Elizabeth
Islands

Ellesmere
Island

GREENLAND
(DENMARK)

Beaufort Sea

Victoria
Island

Baffin
Bay

Baffin
Island

ARCTIC CIRCLE (66°33')

ALASKA
(U.S.)

Great
Bear Lake

Davis
Strait

Denmark
Strait

Reykjavi

Anchorage

Gulf of
Alaska

Juneau

Great
Slave Lake

Churchill

Hudson
Bay

CANADA

Labrador
Sea

NORTH
PACIFIC OCEAN

Vancouver

Seattle

NORTH
AMERICA

Lake
Winnipeg

Great
Lakes

Montréal

Québec

Ottawa

NORTH
ATLANTIC OCEAN

AZORES
(PORTUGAL)

UNITED STATES

Toronto

New York

Chicago

San Francisco

Denver

St. Louis

Washington,
D.C.

Los Angeles

Dallas

Atlanta

BERMUDA
(U.K.)

CANARY ISLANDS
(SPAIN)

WESTERN SAH
(ADMINISTE
BY MORO

TROPIC OF CANCER (23°27')

Monterrey

Gulf of Mexico

Miami

Nassau

THE BAHAMAS

MEXICO

Havana

CUBA

HAITI

DOMINICAN
REPUBLIC

VIRGIN ISLS.
(U.S.)

BRITISH VIRGIN ISLS. (U.K.)

ANGUILLA (U.K.)

HONOLULU

HAWAII
(U.S.)

Mexico
City

Veracruz

Port-au-
Prince

ST. KITTS AND NEVIS

ANTIGUA AND BARBUDA

GUADELOUPE (FR.)

Nouakchott

ATOLL

GUATEMALA

Belmopan

BELIZE

JAMAICA

Kingston

Santo
Domingo

PUERTO RICO
(U.S.)

DOMINICA

MARTINIQUE (FR.)

CAPE VERDE

Dakar

Praia

Guatemala City

HONDURAS

Caribbean
Sea

ST. LUCIA

ST. VINCENT AND

BARBADOS

THE GAMBIA

Banjul

N REEF
(.)

San Salvador

Tegucigalpa

GRENADA

GUINEA-BISSAU

Bissau

EL SALVADOR

NICARAGUA

ARUBA (NETH.)

THE GRENADINES

Port-of-Spain

SIERRA LEO

Conakr

Freetow

PALMYRA ATOLL
(U.S.)

COSTA RICA

Managua

NETHERLANDS
ANTILLES (NETH.)

TRINIDAD AND TOBAGO

San
José

PANAMA

Caracas

KIRITIMATI
(CHRISTMAS ISLAND)

EQUATOR

Panama

VENEZUELA

Georgetown

Paramaribo

Medellín

Bogotá

GUYANA

Cayenne

SURINAME

FRENCH GUIANA
(FR.)

RVIS ISLAND
(U.S.)

Quito

Cali

COLOMBIA

GALAPAGOS ISLANDS
(ECUADOR)

ECUADOR

Manaus

Belém

Iquitos

BRAZIL

MARQUESAS ISLAND
(FR. POLYNESIA)

Recife

FRENCH POLYNESIA (FRANCE)

PERU

SOUTH
AMERICA

LANDS
.)

Lima

Brasília

Cusco

TUAMOTU
ARCHIPELAGO
(FR. POLYNESIA)

La Paz

BOLIVIA

SOCIETY ISLANDS
(FR. POLYNESIA)

Sucre

Rio de
Janeiro

TROPIC OF CAPRICORN (23°27')

TUBUAI ISLANDS
(FR. POLYNESIA)

PITCAIRN ISLANDS
(U.K.)

EASTER
ISLAND
(CHILE)

ISLA SALA
Y GÓMEZ
(CHILE)

Antofagasta

Paraguay

São
Paulo

Asunción

PARAGUAY

SOUTH
ATLANTIC OCEAN

CHILE

JUAN FERNÁNDEZ
ISLANDS
(CHILE)

Santiago

URUGUAY

Buenos Aires

ARGENTINA

La Plata

Montevideo

Bahía
Blanca

SOUTH
PACIFIC OCEAN

FALKLAND ISLANDS
(ADMINISTERED BY U.K.
CLAIMED BY ARGENTINA)

SOUTH GEORGIA AND THE
SOUTH SANDWICH ISLANDS
(ADMINISTERED BY U.K.
CLAIMED BY ARGENTINA)

Punta Arenas

Stanley

Scotia Sea

Drake
Passage

SOUTH ORKNEY ISLANDS
(B.A.T.)

SOUTHERN
OCEAN

Amundsen Sea

Bellingshausen Sea

Weddell Sea

Ross Sea

Ross
Ice Shelf

Ronne
Ice Shelf

Learn more about the Foreign Policy Association at: WWW.FPA.ORG

Take advantage of valuable program resources at: WWW.GREATDECISIONS.ORG

Connect with us online at: WWW.FACEBOOK.COM/GREATDECISIONS

FOREIGN
POLICY
ASSOCIATION
1918

The Foreign Policy Association, the nation's oldest civic-education organization, was founded nearly a century ago. With the motto "An informed public is an educated public," and the belief that America must possess a citizenry knowledgeable in international affairs, FPA has grown into a national educational institution. FPA produces Great Decisions, a discussion program that takes place annually in communities across the country; the Headline Series, a periodic publication that addresses essential topics in foreign policy; and lectures by experts of all stripes. World dignitaries such as Indira Gandhi, Margaret Thatcher, Bill Clinton and Ban Ki-moon have taken the podium at FPA events.

OPINION BALLOTS • 2013

Submit your ballot online at **www.greatdecisions.org**

1 THE EURO

ISSUE A. To what extent do you agree or disagree with the following two statements?

1. U.S. banking regulators should scrutinize European banks that operate in the U.S. more closely.

___ Strongly agree
___ Somewhat agree
___ Somewhat disagree
___ Strongly disagree
___ Not sure

2. U.S. banking regulators should discourage American financial institutions from investing in Europe.

___ Strongly agree
___ Somewhat agree
___ Somewhat disagree
___ Strongly disagree
___ Not sure

(REQUIRED) Your zip code:............................
Date: /   /2013   *Ballot continues on reverse side.*

2 EGYPT

ISSUE A. Which of the following should be the highest priority for the U.S. in Egypt? (Rank in order from 1 to 5, with 1 being the highest.)
___ Building relationships with Islamist politicians
___ Building relationships with the Egyptian military
___ Providing economic aid
___ Preserving regional stability and security
___ Other

ISSUE B. To what extent do you support or oppose the U.S. establishing a free trade agreement with Egypt?
___ Strongly support
___ Somewhat support
___ Somewhat oppose
___ Strongly oppose
___ Not sure

ISSUE C. How much pressure should the U.S. government put on Egypt's new regime to uphold the Camp David accords and maintain good relations with Israel?
___ A great deal of pressure
___ Some pressure
___ Not too much pressure
___ No pressure at all
___ Not sure

(REQUIRED) Your zip code:............................
Date: /   /2013   *Ballot continues on reverse side.*

3 NATO

ISSUE A. To what extent do you agree or disagree with the following statement? NATO faces a crisis in purpose and direction.

___ Strongly agree
___ Somewhat agree
___ Somewhat disagree
___ Strongly disagree
___ Not sure

ISSUE B. To what extent do you agree or disagree with the following statement? The U.S. government should shift its priorities away from NATO and Europe toward other regions and security concerns.

___ Strongly agree
___ Somewhat agree
___ Somewhat disagree
___ Strongly disagree
___ Not sure

(REQUIRED) Your zip code:............................
Date: /   /2013   *Ballot continues on reverse side.*

4 MYANMAR

ISSUE A. Regarding international economic sanctions in Myanmar, to what extent do you agree or disagree with the following two statements?

1. The U.S. should not roll back sanctions further until Myanmar has made more reforms for democratization.

___ Strongly agree
___ Somewhat agree
___ Somewhat disagree
___ Strongly disagree
___ Not sure

2. The democratic reforms undertaken by Myanmar's leadership demonstrate that international sanctions were a successful strategy.

___ Strongly agree
___ Somewhat agree
___ Somewhat disagree
___ Strongly disagree
___ Not sure

(REQUIRED) Your zip code:............................
Date: /   /2013   *Ballot continues on reverse side.*

Please submit only one ballot per person, per topic. Ballots must be received by June 30, 2013.
Mail ballots to: **FOREIGN POLICY ASSOCIATION, 470 Park Avenue South, New York, NY 10016-6819**

ISSUE D. How convincing do you find each of the four arguments below about how the U.S. should reassess its economic aid to Egypt?

	VERY	NOT VERY
1. The U.S. should continue to provide aid to Egypt because it helps Egypt's emerging democracy as it goes through a transition.	❑	❑
2. The U.S. should continue to provide aid because it helps provide stability and is a continuing way for the U.S. to influence events.	❑	❑
3. The U.S. should stop giving aid to the Egyptian government because it has been slow to criticize, and has failed to effectively confront, those who have perpetrated attacks against Americans and the U.S. Embassy in Cairo.	❑	❑
4. Given the difficult economic times the U.S. is going through, it is unwise for the U.S. to give large amounts of aid to Egypt.	❑	❑

So now, do you think U.S. foreign aid to Egypt should be:

____ Increased
____ Kept the same
____ Decreased
____ Not sure

2

ISSUE B. To what extent do you support or oppose the creation of Eurobonds by the European Union?

____ Strongly support
____ Somewhat support
____ Somewhat oppose
____ Strongly oppose
____ Not sure

ISSUE C. Suppose European countries need a bailout to avoid defaulting on their debt. To what extent do you support or oppose the U.S. providing funding to help bailout European countries?

____ Strongly support
____ Somewhat support
____ Somewhat oppose
____ Strongly oppose
____ Not sure

1

ISSUE B. Which of the following issues should be the top priority in U.S. relations with Myanmar? (Rank in order from 1 to 5, with 1 being most important)

____ Fair and free elections
____ Human rights issues, including ethnic minority rights
____ Economic investment
____ The "pivot to Asia" in national security strategy
____ Other:

ISSUE C. To what extent do you support or oppose the U.S. government encouraging private-sector investment and engagement of American firms in Myanmar?

____ Strongly support
____ Somewhat support
____ Somewhat oppose
____ Strongly oppose
____ Not sure

4

ISSUE C. What should be the primary goal shaping the U.S. and NATO's continuing involvement in Afghanistan? (Rank in order from 1 to 6, with 1 the most important)

____ Preventing the country from becoming a sanctuary for terrorists
____ Building a viable democratic state
____ Eradicating the Taliban
____ Increasing economic development
____ Improving the protection of human and women's rights
____ Other

ISSUE D. Do you support or oppose a reduction in U.S. government defense spending, even if doing so significantly reduces NATO's military capacity?

____ Strongly support
____ Somewhat support
____ Somewhat oppose
____ Strongly oppose
____ Not sure

3

5 — INTERVENTION

ISSUE A. To what extent do you agree or disagree with the following statements about the responsibility to protect doctrine? A U.S. military intervention in Syria is justified under the R2P doctrine.

___ Strongly agree
___ Somewhat agree
___ Somewhat disagree
___ Strongly disagree
___ Not sure

ISSUE B. The international intervention in Libya in 2011 was an example of the R2P doctrine well-applied.

___ Strongly agree
___ Somewhat agree
___ Somewhat disagree
___ Strongly disagree
___ Not sure

(REQUIRED) Your zip code:..
Date: / /2013 *Ballot continues on reverse side.*

6 — IRAN

ISSUE A. To what extent do you agree or disagree with the following statement regarding U.S. sanctions against Iran? The economic sanctions against Iran to keep it from building nuclear weapons are working.

___ Strongly agree
___ Somewhat agree
___ Somewhat disagree
___ Strongly disagree
___ Not sure

ISSUE B. When should the U.S. begin to roll back sanctions on Iran?

___ Right now
___ After it reopens nuclear talks
___ After it stops its nuclear program
___ After it holds fair and free elections
___ Other

(REQUIRED) Your zip code:..
Date: / /2013 *Ballot continues on reverse side.*

7 — CHINA IN AFRICA

ISSUE A. What is the most important concern facing the U.S. regarding China in Africa? (Rank from 1 to 6, with 1 most important.)

___ China as a supplier of small arms and light weapons to African countries
___ China's military operations in Africa
___ China's Communist economic system serving as a possible economic model for Africa
___ China's increasing economic cooperation with Africa
___ China's support for undemocratic forms of government
___ Other

ISSUE B. What should be the top U.S. priority in Africa? (Rank in order from 1 to 8, with 1 being the highest priority)

___ Peacekeeping
___ Democracy building
___ Humanitarian assistance
___ Human rights
___ Economic investment
___ Natural resources
___ Trade
___ Other

(REQUIRED) Your zip code:..
Date: / /2013 *Ballot continues on reverse side.*

8 — THREAT ASSESSMENT

ISSUE A. Which of the following represents the greatest threat to the U.S. today? (Rank in order from 1 to 6, with 1 being the greatest threat)

___ China
___ Global health crisis
___ Economic crisis
___ Radical Islamist governments
___ Rogue nuclear states
___ Other

ISSUE B. Which of the following do you think will represent the greatest threat to the U.S. two decades from now? (Rank in order from 1 to 6, with 1 being the greatest threat)

___ China
___ Global health crisis
___ Economic crisis
___ Radical Islamist governments
___ Rogue nuclear states
___ Other

(REQUIRED) Your zip code:..
Date: / /2013 *Ballot continues on reverse side.*

ISSUE C. To what extent do you support or oppose U.S. military cooperation with Israel if Israel launches a preemptive strike against Iran's nuclear program?

___ Strongly support

___ Somewhat support

___ Somewhat oppose

___ Strongly oppose

___ Not sure

ISSUE D. Which of the following represents the best U.S. policy regarding Iran? (Rank in order from 1 to 4, with 1 being the best policy)

___ Military action

___ Diplomatic dialogue

___ Covert actions, e.g., cyberattacks

___ Sanctions

ISSUE C. In addition to being a moral responsibility, R2P is in the national security interests of the U.S.

___ Strongly agree

___ Somewhat agree

___ Somewhat disagree

___ Strongly disagree

___ Not sure

ISSUE D. The U.S. should channel its R2P efforts through the newly created Atrocities Prevention Board.

___ Strongly agree

___ Somewhat agree

___ Somewhat disagree

___ Strongly disagree

___ Not sure

6

5

ISSUE C. To what extent do you agree or disagree with the following statement? The U.S. Senate should pass legislation to regulate national infrastructure in private hands.

___ Strongly agree

___ Somewhat agree

___ Somewhat disagree

___ Strongly disagree

___ Not sure

ISSUE D. To what extent do you agree or disagree with the following statements regarding U.S. policy toward North Korea?

1. The U.S. should continue using economic sanctions to address the threat of a nuclear North Korea.

___ Strongly agree

___ Somewhat agree

___ Somewhat disagree

___ Strongly disagree

___ Not sure

2. The U.S. should continue using multilateral talks to address the threat of a nuclear North Korea.

___ Strongly agree

___ Somewhat agree

___ Somewhat disagree

___ Strongly disagree

___ Not sure

A. *How long have you participated in the GREAT DECISIONS program (i.e., attended one or more discussion sessions)?*
  ❏ This is the first year I have participated.
  ❏ I participated in one previous year.
  ❏ I participated in more than one previous year.

B. *How did you learn about the GREAT DECISIONS program?*
  ❏ Word of mouth ❏ Local library
  ❏ FPA Web site ❏ Organization (indicate below)
  ❏ Promotional brochure _____

C. *Where does your GREAT DECISIONS group meet?*
  ❏ Private home ❏ Library
  ❏ Community center ❏ Learning in Retirement
  ❏ Other:_____

D. *What is your age?* ❏ 17 or under ❏ 18 to 30
  ❏ 31 to 45 ❏ 46 to 60 ❏ 61 or over

E. *Your sex?* ❏ Female ❏ Male

F. *Have you been abroad during the last two years?*
  ❏ Yes ❏ No

G. *Do you know, or are you learning, a foreign language?*
  ❏ Yes ❏ No

H. *What is the highest level of formal education you have completed?* ❏ Some high school
  ❏ High school graduate ❏ Some college
  ❏ College graduate ❏ Advanced degree

I. *How often are you asked for your opinion on foreign policy?*
  ❏ Often ❏ Sometimes ❏ Hardly ever

J. *How many **hours**, on average, do you spend reading one GREAT DECISIONS chapter?* ❏ Less than 1 hr.
  ❏ 1 or 2 hrs. ❏ 3 or 4 hrs. ❏ More than 4 hrs.

K. *Have you changed your opinion in a fairly significant way as a result of taking part in the GREAT DECISIONS program?*
  ❏ Yes ❏ No ❏ Not sure

8

7

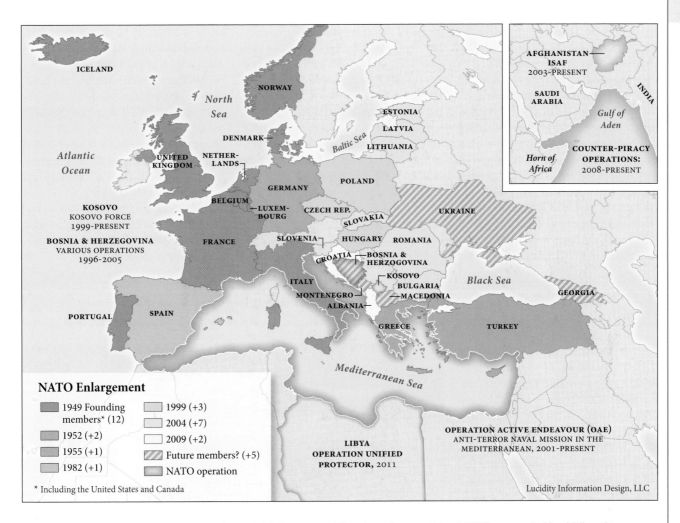

NATO Enlargement

- 1949 Founding members* (12)
- 1952 (+2)
- 1955 (+1)
- 1982 (+1)
- 1999 (+3)
- 2004 (+7)
- 2009 (+2)
- Future members? (+5)
- NATO operation

* Including the United States and Canada

KOSOVO
KOSOVO FORCE
1999-PRESENT

BOSNIA & HERZEGOVINA
VARIOUS OPERATIONS
1996-2005

LIBYA
OPERATION UNIFIED
PROTECTOR, 2011

OPERATION ACTIVE ENDEAVOUR (OAE)
ANTI-TERROR NAVAL MISSION IN THE
MEDITERRANEAN, 2001-PRESENT

AFGHANISTAN—
ISAF
2003-PRESENT

COUNTER-PIRACY
OPERATIONS:
2008-PRESENT

Lucidity Information Design, LLC

---

ability to respond to a broad menu of threats requires forces that are deployable at short notice, functionally flexible, and interoperable with the U.S. To that end, it has pursued a number of initiatives geared toward military modernization and the enhancement of capabilities. The importance of this task was evidenced by the creation in 2003 of Allied Command Transformation (based in Norfolk, Va.) as one of NATO's two strategic commands (Allied Command Operations in Belgium being the other).

For its supporters, it is this adaptive ability that is the mark of NATO's success. In a keynote speech in London in July 2012, NATO Secretary General Anders Fogh Rasmussen argued that Europe and North America could shape a "world that is increasingly unpredictable, complex and interlinked" because of the shared resource of the alliance as "an essential contributor to...international security and stability." Plugging NATO into a rapidly changing world has, however, come at a price. In undertaking missions, the Atlantic alliance has found itself embroiled in conflicts that have been inherently difficult to resolve and that have stretched its capabilities, both material and political, to the limit. In Bosnia, it took a major set of air strikes (Operation Deliberate Force) in 1995 to rescue NATO's fortunes; prior to that point, figures as senior as the U.S. Secretary of State Warren Christopher and NATO's Supreme Allied Commander Europe (SACEUR) had warned that NATO faced redundancy if it failed to stop the war. NATO acted much more expeditiously during the Kosovan crisis of 1999, when the Serbs mercilessly shelled Albanian villages, but here too its credibility was on the line: "[d]emonstrating the seriousness of NATO's purpose" was thus, in President Bill Clinton's words, a key part of the decision to intervene. As for the more recent Libyan campaign of 2011, here NATO succeeded in ridding the country of Muammar el-Qaddafi's regime but was subject to some familiar brickbats. NATO, argued Michael Clarke of the Royal United Services Institute, "was made to look puny in what it could really deploy" and "success...came just in time to save everyone's blushes."

The International Security Assistance Forces (ISAF) mission in Afghanistan is but the latest example of this testing dynamic. NATO's operational experience is, however, only part of the story. The 2010 Strategic Concept outlined three "core tasks" for the Atlantic alliance: "crisis management" (which has accounted for the vast majority of operations), "collective defense" and "cooperative security" through partnerships. None of these lack substance but, when taken together, concerns have arisen over prioritization and focus. Hence, the Strategic Concept occasioned considerable debate within NATO. The American-British preference for a flexible NATO was somewhat at odds with the views of Norway, Poland and the Baltic states who (with an eye to Russia) were keen not to dilute NATO's commitment to traditional territorial defense. That view is shared by some commentators who are concerned that NATO's remit has extended too far. In confronting a world of risk, NATO, they argue, has undertaken functional expansion rather than functional specialization. NATO's consensus decisionmaking procedures have not helped – encouraging a generous, but arguably unfocused, cataloguing of tasks as a

means of satisfying the maximum number of allies. Consequently, it has been suggested, the 2010 Strategic Concept reads more like a descriptive wish list than a compelling vision of strategic, political or even moral direction.

The recent development of the alliance has thus given rise to a range of views. It is clear that NATO has gone well beyond its origins as a military alliance to develop as a multipurpose security organization. That trajectory of development has meant an expansion of both the functional and geographic range of NATO activities, although no

explicit limit has been specified as to how far that range should stretch. Such ambiguity is helpful insofar as it allows the alliance considerable latitude to act or—as the current political crisis in Syria illustrates—not to act. NATO's range, in other words, is determined on a case-by-case basis. The upshot is that NATO has tended to draw lessons from major episodes of operational engagement. Operations in Bosnia and Kosovo during the 1990's thus determined NATO's move out of area; the more recent Afghan campaign may well herald a strategic retreat. ■

What about Afghanistan?

IMPLEMENTING the mandate of the ISAF in Afghanistan has proven to be NATO's most difficult mission to date. For the U.S., commitments to ISAF and to a separate non-NATO undertaking, Operation Enduring Freedom-Afghanistan (OEF-A), have embroiled the country in what *Washington Post* journalist Rajiv Chandrasekaran has labelled the "longest [...] and by far the most complicated war" in American history.

Getting out...

American military involvement in Afghanistan dates back to the months following Sept. 11, when it led an international coalition of the willing (supported by the Afghan Northern Alliance) to oust the Taliban from power and rid the country of al-Qaeda. NATO became a formal party to the post-Taliban stabilization and reconstruction effort in August 2003, having assumed command of ISAF, a body established by the 2001 Bonn Agreement and, under United Nations Security Council Resolution (UNSCR) 1386 (2001), mandated to maintain security in the capital of Kabul and surrounding areas. UNSCR 1510 (2003) extended ISAF's role to the rest of the country while the 2004 Berlin Agreement committed NATO to remain in Afghanistan until the Afghan National Security Forces (ANSF) were "sufficiently constituted and operational." By October 2006, ISAF had

U.S. troops under ISAF patrol with armored vehicles in Arghandab district in southern Afghanistan, a former stronghold of Taliban insurgents. (ROMEO GACAD/AFP/GETTY IMAGES)

been rolled out across the whole country. NATO Operation Plan (OPLAN) 10302 (December 2005) saw ISAF military operations as supporting "the Afghan government in the maintenance of security," facilitating the extension of Afghan government structures and providing an environment conducive to "reconstruction/humanitarian efforts" being undertaken by external agencies. It looked forward to a "self-sustaining, moderate and democratic Afghan government able to exercise its sovereign authority" throughout the country. Up until the mid-2000's, ISAF

had had to contend with only limited resistance. From 2006, however, the insurgency increased markedly. In response, NATO undertook several significant steps. It streamlined its command structures involving (with U.S. cooperation) greater coordination with OEF-A, put a greater emphasis on training the nascent Afghan army and police, and endorsed a move toward a more explicit counter-insurgency strategy. These measures still envisaged a transition to Afghan responsibility for security but, in parallel, meant a ramping up of allied commitment.

This more robust approach was extended by President Obama's administration. U.S. force levels in Afghanistan, which stood at 32,000 personnel at the end of 2008, climbed to nearly 100,000 by the middle of 2011. America's partners also stepped up their efforts during this period with ISAF (minus the U.S. contribution) increasing from approximately 31,000 to just over 42,000 boots on the ground. Intervention, however, came at a price. ISAF fatalities increased year-on-year between 2006 and 2010. A dip in 2011 did little to mask a horrendous toll in lives: 2,750 ISAF dead by the end of 2011, just under two thirds of them American. The material outlay was equally burdensome. The American (and British) drawdown in Iraq had made the cost of the Afghan operation somewhat more tolerable, but after fiscal year 2009 it rose to gargantuan levels. War funding for Afghanistan had cost the U.S. a total of $443 billion by the end of 2011. NATO allies were also feeling the strain. Britain, for instance, had spent approximately £13.5 billion on the campaign by 2011. Politically too, Afghanistan had become a headache. Public opinion within key allies took a decisive swing away from support of the war effort. Meanwhile, within NATO, normally close and cooperative allies quarrelled over tactics (the British and Americans experienced a well-reported falling out in Helmand Province) and a corrosive debate opened up over risk-sharing. The well-established NATO practice of national caveats (that is, restrictions on how, when and where troops are deployed) was used freely by risk-averse nations such as Germany, Italy and Spain even when they had deployed relatively large numbers of troops. Others (for instance, Belgium, Portugal and Norway) were both intolerant of putting their forces in harm's way and unwilling to send them to Afghanistan in reasonable numbers in the first place. In the U.S., this state of affairs was especially frowned upon. What use, Defense Secretary Robert Gates asked in February 2008, was a "two-tiered alliance" in which "some allies [are] willing to fight and die

NATO Secretary General Anders Fogh Rasmussen addresses a news conference during the 2012 Chicago summit. (KEVORK DJANSEZIAN/GETTY IMAGES)

[... and] others [...] are not." Such a situation, he continued, "puts a cloud over the future of the alliance." And overarching all of this was a division over priorities. NATO had done a good job of orchestrating a political consensus to sustain its mission over many years but this belied a lack of agreement on exactly what NATO was doing in Afghanistan. The alliance, as a report of the British House of Commons Defence Committee noted in 2008, was split between governments such as those in Germany, Spain and Italy who felt "NATO's overriding concern should be [...] reconstruction and development" and those more militarily robust allies (the British, Canadians, Dutch and Danes, as well as the Americans) who were committed first and foremost to kinetic operations and counter-insurgency as a means of ensuring any such efforts succeeded.

What made these various pressures worse was a sense that the collective effort in Afghanistan had stalemated. Then newly-appointed, ISAF Commander (and head of U.S. forces in Afghanistan) General Stanley McChrystal, concluded in September 2009 that the "overall situation" in Afghanistan "is deteriorating"—"neither success nor failure [could] be taken for granted." This assessment alluded less to the possibility of a NATO defeat and more to

the impossibility of victory over the Taliban and other Afghan and Pakistan-based insurgents. Further, NATO strategy had by that point become closely associated with the fortunes of the presidency of Hamid Karzai, a character mistrusted in Washington and other NATO capitals, and deeply unpopular throughout Afghanistan itself.

There was, then, growing pressure for a strategic exit from Afghanistan even while NATO and U.S. forces were being ramped up. President Obama's West Point speech of December 2009 announcing the Afghan surge thus conditioned it upon a timetable for American withdrawal and a determination to transfer responsibility for security to the Afghan government. NATO's Lisbon summit of November 2010 extended that approach to the alliance as a whole and foresaw a staged transition by the end of 2014. The Chicago summit of May 2012 declared emphatically that "ISAF's mission will be concluded by the end of 2014." In a clear sign of intent, the U.S. announced in September 2012 that the 33,000 surge troops sent to Afghanistan had already been withdrawn.

...Or staying in?

The transition to the 2014 deadline and the shape of NATO's post-ISAF role pose some fundamental challenges.

A soldier of the German military police overlooks the training of Afghan police officers in Faizabad, northern Afghanistan. (MICHAEL KAPPELER/AFP/GETTY IMAGES)

First, allied solidarity will continue to be tested. "In together, out together" is a touchstone principle of NATO operations, but key allies have already made unilateral and divergent declarations of intent. The Netherlands and Canada, two one-time stalwart ISAF contributors, ended their combat missions in August 2010 and December 2011 respectively. Newly-elected French president Françoise Hollande, meanwhile, made good on a campaign pledge by announcing at Chicago that the entire French combat mission would be withdrawn by year end. Although not unexpected, the move was met with dismay in both London and Washington, where withdrawal has been premised on the retention of a significant combat-capable presence throughout 2013 followed by a rapid drawdown in 2014.

Second, the logistics of withdrawal are hugely complex and politically fraught. The combined NATO nations have to remove over 100,000 armed personnel along with huge stocks of equipment (an estimated 122,000 shipping containers and 70,000 vehicles for ISAF as a whole). Afghanistan's geographic location makes that job much more difficult than the retreat from Iraq or, indeed, the Soviet withdrawal from Afghanistan in 1989 (Moscow could rely on safe passage northward through the Central Asian republics of the then USSR). None of NATO's options are straightforward. It has reverse transit agreements with Russia along with Kazakhstan, Kyrgyzstan and Uzbekistan, which will facilitate land evacuation through the Northern Distribution Route; these same countries also permit U.S. and ISAF forces over-flight rights. However, Russia at present does not allow the transit of lethal equipment and the routes are, in any case, both very long (terminating at ports in Latvia and Georgia) and expensive. The shorter route via Pakistan to the port of Karachi has served as the main artery of equipment moving into Afghanistan and is the most convenient route out. It is, however, politically friable; the Pakistani authorities shut it down from November 2011 to July 2012 following a dispute with the U.S. over the deaths of 24 Pakistani soldiers in a "friendly fire" incident. The sheer scale of the operation may mean a "logistics surge" of personnel in 2014, and even beyond, dedicated to sorting out the removal of equipment. Other less palatable options include gifting supplies to the ANSF, selling equipment to Central Asian governments, or destruction and abandonment. These logistical problems are likely to add to intra-alliance tensions. As British journalist Francis Tusa noted in evidence to the British House of Commons Defence Committee in June 2012, "if everyone is heading for the door at the same time, there will be a scrabble for commercial transport assets, be they trucks from local transporters or aircraft. In that case, you end up in a bidding war with everyone trying to outbid everyone else for the same assets." That France is seeking to leave early already gives it an advantage in obtaining these scare resources.

Third, NATO has to engineer a post-ISAF mission. In the U.S., understandably, debate has centered on what the transition to 2014 and beyond means for American military commitment. But there is a NATO dimension to this too; the vast majority of troops in Afghanistan (American included) are, after all, badged to ISAF. NATO had committed itself to a long-term relationship with Afghanistan with the signing of an Enduring Partnership agreement in November 2010. A Declaration on Afghanistan adopted at Chicago, meanwhile, noted that NATO will shift "from a combat mission to a new training, advising and assistance mission." "Afghanistan," it declared, "will not stand alone; we reaffirm that our close partnership will continue beyond the end of the transition period." At Chicago, agreement was also reached on an American plan for funding the ANSF through to 2024 that would involve coordinated contributions from NATO allies (the lion's share provided by the U.S.) with the proportion slated to come from the Afghan authorities increasing over time. The exact shape of the NATO mission in support of the ANSF, however, remains unclear as of this writing. At a press briefing in late July 2012 Major General Stephen Day (ISAF Deputy Chief of Staff Plans) noted that it was "still [the] subject of debate in nations' capitals." It is not intended to focus principally on combat and NATO has also announced the winding up of its Provincial Reconstruction Teams (PRTs) after 2014. Sten Rynning, in one of the few analyses of the post-ISAF mission, has suggested that the most likely scenario is a repackaging of the NATO Training Mission-Afghanistan (NTM-A) established in 2009. This will likely be headquartered in Kabul, but to be effective will entail a field presence in Afghanistan's major cities. That will expose NATO trainers to the threat of attack by insurgents and so (in the absence of reliable Afghan protection) will require robust rules of engagement and the presence of rapid reaction rescue forces. In that sense, NATO post-ISAF would retain a residual combat function. As Senator Karl Levin noted in hearings of the Armed Services Committee in March 2012, that force will also require "coalition support in key enablers such as logistics, airlift and intelligence support."

It is too early to identify the in-country contributions to training the ANSF from among NATO nations after 2014. NTM-A to date has been staffed mainly by British, French, Canadian, Turkish and American personnel with a significant Italian and German presence dedicated to the police training aspect of the mission. Britain, France and Germany all signed strategic partnership agreements with the Afghan authorities in early 2012, and in July Britain signed a memorandum of understanding to support an Afghan National Army Officer Academy. As for the U.S., it is likely to contribute to the post-ISAF mission, although it may not lead it. At present a U.S. command sergeant major leads NTM-A, and since 2007 a succession of U.S. generals have commanded ISAF. During its early years, however, ISAF was led by high-ranking officers from the British, German, Italian and Turkish armed forces. Should the European component to the post-ISAF mission be significant, that approach may well be returned to. This is not to say, of course, that the U.S. presence in Afghanistan will be inconsequential. The U.S.-Afghanistan Strategic Partnership Agreement of May 2012 foresees "long-term strategic cooperation" until 2024 and, in that context, Afghanistan has been designated a "Major Non-NATO Ally" of the U.S. More specifically, the U.S. is likely to continue with its own (non-NATO) training effort, the Combined Security Transition Command-Afghanistan, and retain after 2014 an ongoing counterterror operation in Afghanistan

and Pakistan waged through special operations on land and drone strikes from the air. That mission, an extension of OEF-A, could conceivably involve partner countries (Britain is reportedly planning special forces operations after 2014 in Afghanistan) but, just like OEF-A, NATO would have no formal oversight or chain of command.

The fourth challenge to NATO in Afghanistan is one of credibility. The 2014 deadline has imposed a very stern test upon the alliance and it could wreck its reputation as a global security actor if the withdrawal leaves behind a country in turmoil. NATO and its main allies have already lowered their ambitions both on what ISAF has achieved to date and what the goals for success in Afghanistan are in the future. The Chicago Declaration on Afghanistan did refer in glowing terms to economic, social and political progress over a decade but went on to stress that ISAF's role was now to promote Afghan self-reliance. President Obama has been even more direct in this regard, announcing in May 2012 that America's "goal is not to build a country in America's image, or to eradicate every vestige of the Taliban." Such objectives, he continued, "would require many more years, many more dollars, and most impor-

tantly, many more American lives. Our goal is to destroy al-Qaeda, and we are on a path to do exactly that." Reports of thinking within the administration since the Chicago summit suggest it has settled for a goal of "Afghan good enough," an assumption that by 2014 the U.S. will be supporting a serviceable government and Afghan armed forces able to keep the Taliban at bay in Kabul and the north of the country but resigned to a loss of control across the Pashtun south, where Taliban, Haqqani and other insurgents will, if necessary, be dealt with by special forces. Such a state of affairs would be a return to American and allied goals immediately after Sept. 11 — namely, to keep the Taliban out of power and prevent Afghanistan from becoming an al-Qaeda sanctuary. Such an approach has crossed party lines in the U.S. Afghanistan did not figure large in the 2012 presidential election debates, and President Obama's challenger, Governor Mitt Romney, offered very little that was different from the policy of the incumbent. Some qualification was offered on the firmness of the 2014 withdrawal deadline (Romney said he would first seek the advice of commanders on the ground), but the commitment to a reduced American and NATO footprint in the long term is shared by both Demo-

Oil tankers used to transport fuel to NATO forces in Afghanistan are seen at a NATO supply terminal in the southern Pakistani port city of Karachi in July 2012, after Pakistan had announced it was reopening land routes for NATO forces in neighboring Afghanistan.
(MASROOR/XINHUA/EYEVINE/REDUX)

crats and Republicans. Versions of that same narrative, furthermore, have been heard for some time in London, Paris and other NATO capitals.

Pragmatic realism of this sort is reinforced by two claims from within NATO: first, that the insurgency is being degraded and, second, that the ANSF is on target to take over a comprehensive security lead in Afghanistan in line with the ISAF timetable. Both have been subject to considerable scrutiny, and expert opinion is divided in judging the resilience of the insur-

mate, meanwhile, courts disaster as it embroils the U.S. in an interminable conflict, creates pressure for an open-ended post-ISAF mission, and destabilizes Pakistan. Part of the solution for Lieven and others is the pursuit of a negotiated political settlement between Kabul and the insurgency. That, in principle, is not unwelcome in Washington. Secretary of State Hillary Clinton announced in February 2011 a "diplomatic surge" to complement the military campaign. Efforts as of 2012, however, had yielded little. Pakistan has proven

country in October 2012. What, then, can be concluded? The key points for NATO, most objective commentators seem to agree, can be boiled down to the following:

■ Until it issued a "strategic vision" for Afghanistan in 2008, NATO was directionless and reactive. At that point the U.S. (and to a degree Britain) shifted their strategic sights away from Iraq to Afghanistan. The resultant U.S. troop surge in Afghanistan was accompanied in NATO by greater unity of command and sense of purpose—even if that purpose was premised above all on executing a viable exit strategy.

■ Afghanistan has been the site of NATO's first, and so far only, experience of coalition counterinsurgency and expeditionary warfare. The outcome has been far from ideal, but the alliance has proven flexible in its ability to mount, sustain and adapt multinational operations in a hostile environment and at a distance.

■ Mission failure has been avoided to date and NATO has dug deep into its political reserves to sustain consensus and maintain commitment.

■ NATO, building on earlier experiences in Bosnia and Kosovo, has worked hard to integrate a civilian element to its work in Afghanistan (through PRTs and advice to the civilian components of the Afghan ministries of defense and interior).

■ The prolonged and intense experience of working together in combat settings has facilitated the development of NATO joint doctrine on operations, counterinsurgency and civil-military cooperation.

■ NATO (and, by extension, the U.S.) has gained valuable experience in working with non-NATO partners. ISAF, while NATO-led, is an international coalition that in mid-2012 consisted of 50 participating nations. Some—Australia, Georgia, Sweden, South Korea—have made significant troop contributions. Partnerships, however, have not always worked well. That with the 27-member European Union (EU), despite extensive overlap of membership with NATO, has proven particularly disappointing.

President Obama walks alongside NATO Secretary General Anders Fogh Rasmussen, with other heads of state, at NATO's 2012 summit in Chicago. (SAUL LOEB/AFP/GETTY IMAGES)

gency and the readiness of the ANSF to take it on as NATO withdraws. But beyond this debate is a much bigger question: how determined are the U.S. and its allies to see through a real and lasting stabilization of Afghanistan? NATO risks throwing away more than 10 years' investment of lives, money and political credibility. As Anatol Lieven, Professor of War Studies at Kings College London, has argued, a flight from Afghanistan "would be seen purely as a response to Western losses, reflect callous disregard for the plight of the Afghan people, and lead to justified feelings of triumph on the part of the Taliban and their allies." Seeking some sort of tolerable military stale-

an unreliable go-between, the Taliban an often inaccessible interlocutor, and the Obama administration unwilling to appear conciliatory in the run-up to the 2012 US presidential election.

Lessons of Afghanistan

Given the divisiveness of the Afghan experience and the uncertainty of the outcome, it would be easy to see NATO's involvement in Afghanistan in a largely negative light. The message put out by the alliance, by contrast, is determinedly upbeat: NATO has a viable plan "to build long-term security for the Afghans, the wider region and ourselves," Secretary General Rasmussen noted during a visit to the

■ NATO in Afghanistan has functioned, according to military operations researcher Alexander Mattelaer, as "a platform for coalitions of members and nonmembers alike." NATO's "greatest asset," he continues, "is its permanent command chain [...and] culture of interoperability." This "enabling function" is unique as a facilitator of multilateral operations and "perhaps the best guarantee of NATO's continued existence."

None of these points is meant to suggest that NATO would welcome a repeat of a mission as trying as ISAF. They do, however, reaffirm the staying power of the alliance. The experience of Afghanistan will not mean the "the end of the alliance" as some analysts once predicted. How, then, will NATO develop as the Afghan mission is wound down? ■

Looking ahead at NATO

NATO HAS OVER the last decade adopted a wide-ranging set of tasks. But in what sense has it become a global body? In this connection, it is worth considering two very important limitations. First, no one in policy circles regards the alliance as open to members beyond the Euro-Atlantic area. That possibility, often accredited to a widely cited article coauthored by James Goldgeier and Ivo Daalder, gained currency in the mid-2000's as a means of consolidating the important contribution to NATO operations by states such as Australia, South Korea and Japan. None of these countries, however, has shown any enthusiasm for membership and the idea has, in any case, run foul of the broader politics of enlargement. The alliance has admitted 12 new members since the end of the cold war but has lost interest in continuing the process even within Europe. Macedonian accession has been blocked by Greece, and the efforts of President George W. Bush's administration to facilitate Georgian membership were thwarted by Germany and France at NATO's Bucharest summit in 2008. France and Turkey are particularly skeptical of extending NATO membership beyond Europe, and the Obama administration (including Daalder, who was elevated to the post of U.S. permanent representative to NATO in May 2009) has not pursued the matter.

Second, NATO is not seen as a substitute for the United Nations. For different reasons, France, Britain and the U.S. (NATO allies who are all permanent members of the Security Council) regard that body as serving important functions quite distinct from the alliance. The United Nations is the princi-

A crew member at work inside a NATO Airborne Warning and Control System (AWACS) while flying over the Mediterranean sea during the NATO Operation Unified Protector over Libya in 2011. (ALBERTO PIZZOLI/AFP/GETTY IMAGES)

pal source of international legitimacy in global affairs and still the main vehicle for dialogue with Russia and China on international problems. Iran, Syria and North Korea—states at the top of America's list of current concerns—do not generally figure in NATO-Russia discussions and concrete action, such as it is on these matters, has followed United Nations routes (at the Security Council, Russia has blocked efforts to impose sanctions on Syria but has approved them in the cases of Iran and North Korea).

Given these political sensitivities, the meaning of NATO's global remit has been difficult to pin down. In a rather awkward phrase, Secretary General Rasmussen has referred to the alliance as assuming a "global perspective" but not permanent "global responsibilities." That "perspective" has a number of manifestations. For many allies, the main threats they face are located close to home (attitudes toward Russia were noted above, and NATO member Turkey sits aside the turbulent states of Syria and Iraq). However, there is a common appreciation also that NATO's "security environment" is global in scale. Threats such as terrorism, cyberthreats and piracy on the high seas are all mentioned in the Strategic Concept; these are truly transnational in origin and effect, and through its command and planning mechanisms NATO has set out ways of addressing them all. Further, NATO is still the world's most capable collective body for integrated military response, and over the last decade it has deployed further and further afield. Afghanistan has hogged the headlines, but NATO has since 2001 sustained Operation Active Endeavour (OAE),

Smoke billows over Tripoli in March 2011 after a NATO-led coalition air strike. (MAHMUD TURKIA/AFP/GETTY IMAGES)

a counterterrorist naval mission in the Mediterranean, as well as a counterpiracy flotilla off the Horn of Africa since 2008 and a mission in support of the 53-member African Union (AU) since 2007. Kosovo Force (KFOR), first deployed in 1999, remains active to this day. NATO has also undertaken small-scale humanitarian missions in Haiti and Pakistan, and in 2011 mounted Operation Unified Protector (OUP), a major armed intervention in Libya.

The merit of NATO's broad agenda is that it keeps the organization relevant to the security challenges of the age of globalization. But this also brings problems. The more security challenges NATO sees as relevant, the more, ironically, it internalizes a sense of being under threat. The issues this raises are both conceptual and practical. If NATO is alert to cybersecurity, for instance, should an attack on a member fall under the purview of the collective defense provisions of Article 5 of the founding North Atlantic Treaty, even though there would have been no loss of life or infringement of territory? Further, with

so many tasks to attend to, what is the proper mix of forces and structures of command? In that regard, NATO made public in Chicago its long-awaited "Deterrence and Defence Posture Review." That document overviewed NATO's conventional, nuclear and missile defense capabilities, but concluded unremarkably that "in the current circumstances, the existing mix of capabilities and the plans for their development are sound," thus leaving unanswered one of the lasting legacies of the cold war: What role precisely do nuclear weapons serve in the alliance and against whom are they directed?

That question has an indirect but nonetheless significant bearing on NATO's prospects as a global body. NATO has developed global partnerships either out of urgent necessity (as in the cases of Afghanistan and Pakistan) or because certain countries have proved themselves reliable allies in operations (Australia). NATO, however, still lacks meaningful relations with major powers such as China and India and, among the BRIC countries (Brazil, Russia, India and China) as a whole. Only Russia has been involved in extended cooperation. Moscow occupies a privileged position by virtue of the 1997 NATO-Russia Founding Act and the work of the NATO-Russia Council. Yet relations have long been bumpy. Cooperation has occurred over Afghanistan and in the Balkans, but Russia has been a vocal opponent of enlargement, has suspended its participation in the Conventional Forces in Europe Treaty and in 2008 went to war with Georgia, a close partner of the alliance. Blame for that war remains disputed, but Russia had long been aggrieved by Georgia's ambitions to join NATO and saw on this occasion an opportunity to prevent it through military destabilization. But hanging over all of this is a legacy question of nuclear strategy. Iranian nuclear ambitions may be the publicly stated reason for NATO's missile defense project but Russia is the only nuclear power that can presently rival the U.S. and the only one that poses, however hypothetical, a direct threat to Europe. It is thus, by default, the main

KFOR soldiers guard a road between the north and south parts of the town of Mitrovica, during clashes in the town of Zvecan, Serbia in June 2012. (EPA/CORBIS)

object of American extended nuclear deterrence in NATO.

For all this, NATO has learned to live with Russia. A pragmatic if prickly relationship does not help NATO's global agenda but neither does it preclude it. The biggest obstacle in this regard is, in fact, the capacity of NATO states themselves.

NATO in an age of defense austerity

The broadening of NATO's remit has not been met with any increase in resources; in fact, the reverse. The global financial crisis since 2008 has required cuts to fiscal deficits among almost all the allies and this, in turn, has entailed significant reductions in defense spending. The London-based International Institute for Strategic Studies recently reported that real defense expenditures in NATO Europe fell by 7.4 percent between 2008 and 2010. Europe's most significant military powers—France, Germany, Italy and Britain—are all due to slash budgets still further in the years ahead. In the U.S., meanwhile, a 10-year hike in military expenditures will be reversed under the terms of the 2011 Budget Control Act, with planned cuts of $487 billion by 2021. Sequestration (the process by which cuts are multiplied in the absence of an agreed federal budget) could potentially double that figure.

The amounts sound truly colossal but the U.S. is beginning from a very high starting point. Even allowing for significant increases in defense spending in China and Russia, the U.S. will remain for the foreseeable future the world's preeminent power. In 2011 it accounted for 45.7 percent of global military expenditure compared to China's 5.5 percent, a gap that will take decades to close, even if one assumes current Chinese growth projections continue. Further, NATO's aggregated military power remains formidable. In 2011, the U.S., Britain, France and Germany were ranked respectively the world's first, third, fourth and eighth largest military spenders.

Yet cuts will inevitably have an effect. A report of the NATO Parliamentary Assembly recently noted that while

New Afghan police officers attend their graduation ceremony in Kabul. (AHMAD MASSOUD/ XINHUA/EYEVINE/REDUX)

"NATO will remain the most powerful alliance in the world, it will have to wield its power more selectively and carefully." Reductions in France and Britain (home of Europe's most able expeditionary forces) are likely to deplete the capabilities necessary for force-projection missions so that these states will be capable of mounting only one reasonably-sized and time-limited expeditionary mission at a time, a state of affairs that would rule out a repeat of the protracted counterinsurgency effort in Afghanistan. NATO's European states would still be capable of less-demanding missions close to home (naval patrols in the Mediterranean or off African coasts) and even of undertaking intense kinetic operations such as that waged in Libya (so long as this was in Europe's neighborhood and accompanied by American participation). However, the risk of overcommitment and a thinning of forces will henceforth be that much greater.

Austerity is a political as well as an operational matter. Falling budgets exacerbate burden-sharing problems and threaten to undermine cohesion and solidarity. Defense budgets, furthermore, are a national, not a NATO, prerogative. The alliance has already undertaken a reform of its command structures and agencies but because it possesses few

Dutch NATO soldiers freed 20 Yemeni hostages and briefly detained seven pirates off the coast of Somalia. The pirates had forced the Yemenis to sail a "mother ship" attacking vessels in the Gulf of Aden. (HO/REUTERS/CORBIS)

Lord Ismay, the first secretary-general of NATO, inspects an honor guard of Portuguese troops in 1954.(BETTMANN/CORBIS)

assets of its own, it cannot determine the course that national defense-spending cuts will take. The fear is, therefore, that these will be driven by local economic exigencies with no coordination or shared purpose. To address that problem the alliance announced in Chicago two key initiatives under the umbrella of "NATO Forces 2020": Smart Defence and the Connected Forces Initiative. These have laudable objectives—to enhance collaborative defense efforts within the alliance—but such initiatives will at best only mitigate (not reverse) the operational consequences of constrained defense spending.

A lessened American presence

NATO's development has always been shaped, in large measure, by the priorities and leadership of the U.S. That will continue but the American attitude has become increasingly hard-nosed and contingent. Policy options for the U.S. will be framed by three key drivers that have become clear under the Obama administration.

First, the U.S. has, over a lengthy period of time, lowered the strategic importance it places upon Europe. That shift has certain milestones of which the end of the cold war, Sept. 11 and the launch of wars in Iraq and Afghanistan are the most obvious. The Department of Defense Strategic Guidance published in January 2012 reaffirmed the trend by endorsing a strategic "pivot" of the U.S. military toward the Asia-Pacific, not least because of concerns about the rise of China. This does not mean the U.S. will lose interest in Europe. U.S. force reductions will strip out two brigades from Germany by 2017, but the U.S. will still retain close to 70,000 troops on the Continent. Institutionally, that presence only partly benefits NATO (U.S. military engagement in Europe is mainly routed through U.S. European Command [EUCOM] and not NATO's Supreme Headquarters Allied Powers Europe [SHAPE]), yet it is still a sign of commitment to the allies. The U.S. contribution to NATO missile defense and even the seemingly anachronistic presence of U.S. short-range nuclear weapons in some NATO countries adds further reassurance. A forward presence in Europe is also of considerable benefit to the U.S. Bases in Britain, Germany and elsewhere remain useful staging posts for U.S. operations in the greater Middle East and,

as John Deni of the U.S. Army War College has argued, American personnel on the Continent now have as their principal purpose "the maintenance of interoperability with Washington's most capable [and] newest... allies and partners."

Second, while the U.S. clearly benefits from a concentration of allies, it has nonetheless become increasingly disillusioned at what it perceives as free-riding within NATO. In a widely reported speech, the outgoing Secretary of Defense Gates warned in June 2011 that "the decline of European defense capabilities" meant that American leaders "may not consider the return on America's investment in NATO worth the cost." The U.S. has borne a disproportionate share of allied defense spending for decades and such complaints have been heard many times before. This time, however, the situation is more pressing as the U.S. itself seeks to cut back on its defense budget. The trans-Atlantic spending gap has had severe operational consequences. The difficulties of European allies working alongside the U.S. were evident as far back as Operation Desert Storm in 1991, and NATO operations in Kosovo and Libya revealed further problems. But it has been Afghanistan which has led to unprecedented levels of unease in the U.S. This is not just a question of sharing the risk, but also of having forces capable and modern enough to serve alongside the American military. As the Afghan priority is superseded by others, that question will stay in the fore. The 2012 Strategic Guidance does allow for the U.S. to partner "with Europeans on global security missions," but a NATO role in assisting with military contingencies in the Asia-Pacific is not at present a serious option (NATO is instead limited to a largely political function working in parallel with the U.S. in consolidating relationships with regional allies such as Australia, Japan and South Korea).

American policy is thus premised on a NATO that is less operationally ambitious and more focused on Europe's neighborhood. That role for NATO is the third driver of change. European states are not averse to stepping up to this challenge. Within the alliance, a European pillar was developed during the 1990's and NATO has since 1992 housed the Allied Rapid Reaction Corps under British leadership. The bulk of personnel for NATO peacekeeping missions in Bosnia and Kosovo have been provided by European nations, and OAE is carried out using Spanish, Greek, Italian and Turkish vessels. If the alliance is headed for a significant rebalancing of effort, this could well mean the development of what Ellen Hallams and Benjamin Schreer have referred to as a "post-American" NATO—not an alliance without the U.S., but one in which American engagement will be that much more discriminating. This will not entail a removal of America's guarantee to the defense of Europe, NATO's core mission. Neither will it mean the U.S. absenting itself entirely from operations (the U.S., as in the Libyan operation, can still play the role of a key enabler providing planners, and surveillance, intelligence and targeting data). It will, however, mean a U.S. unwilling to lead in wars of choice in or around Europe. And in this connection, questions abound. Where, most importantly, will European leadership come from? The contenders are few in number. Germany and Turkey are, for different reasons, reluctant to assume a role that puts them in the front of military action, while the more interventionist France and Britain are, as has been shown, engaged in a process of austerity-driven strategic retrenchment. And even if London and Paris do step up to a greater role (as they did in OUP in Libya), NATO might then see a repeat of burden-sharing debates, this time within Europe rather than across the Atlantic. What would that do for alliance solidarity? Further, the notion of European leadership is itself antithetical to NATO. The alliance is, after all, an organization that defers to the U.S. politically as well as militarily, and only occasionally does a European leader rise above the fray (as Britain's Tony Blair did over Kosovo or France's Nicolas Sarkozy did over Libya). If the U.S. is unwilling to become involved

U.S., Russian, Turkish, Dutch and Danish soldiers participated in NATO's Stabilization Force in Bosnia (SFOR). (DAMIR SAGOLI/REUTERS/CORBIS)

and a European lead is absent, missions may not occur at all, a pattern already in evidence in NATO's sitting out the conflict in Syria. Does an absence of U.S. leadership in the alliance, therefore, simply condemn NATO to impotence?

In conclusion

A NATO with reduced American leadership will converge with other trends. NATO, according to Jamie P. Shea, its deputy assistant secretary-general for emerging security challenges, "could soon be an alliance without a major operation." The wars in Iraq and Afghanistan have neutered any American desire for future land-based expeditionary missions. And among the allies there is even less enthusiasm. Iraq was not a NATO mission (too many allies opposed the intervention) and as Daniel Keohane of the Madrid-based think tank, FRIDE, has argued, "[m]ost Europeans went to Afghanistan for the sake of their close relationship with the U.S., not because they felt it was an existential threat to their security." As a legacy of ISAF, NATO will remain in some (diminishing) form in Afghanistan for many years. NATO will also retain an international network of political relationships and entertain sustainable,

non-kinetic missions far from home. Kinetic, or combat, missions, if they do occur, will be short in duration and (for it to be a NATO mission, rather than an American-led coalition of the willing) in or close to Europe. NATO is developing capabilities for dealing with the wide range of security challenges identified in its latest Strategic Concept and retains an infrastructure of joint planning and a "toolbox" of interoperable capabilities and military experience that is unrivaled. It is an open question, whether that is enough to sustain NATO's relevance. But it would be worse to let the alliance slip into a state of benign neglect. This, for all the language of pessimism that surrounds the organization, seems to be appreciated on both sides of the Atlantic. NATO has been said to be in crisis for much of its life span, but no ally has left, and it structures, strategy and missions have proved durable and adaptable. Even in an era of retrenchment, NATO, for its supporters, is the best there is, if should Europeans, Canadians and Americans need to act together. ∎

✔ **Opinion Ballots**
after page 32

discussion questions

1. Consider NATO's founding principles. How has NATO's mission changed since the cold war? What kind of operations characterized the 1990's? What kind of concerns guide NATO's missions today? How has NATO adapted to the changing geopolitical order?

2. Why is NATO seen to be in crisis? What explains the ability of the alliance to ride crises out and survive?

3. What role has NATO played in Afghanistan since 2001? How has its mission in the country changed over time and what is the nature of its exit strategy? In what ways has the mission impacted the political and military development of the alliance?

4. NATO's 2010 Strategic Concept refers to the "core tasks" of the alliance as collective defense, crisis management and cooperative security. How do these priorities differ? What policies does NATO pursue in order to achieve them?

5. How has defense austerity impacted the U.S. and its NATO allies? Will defense cuts affect the ability of NATO to carry out its core tasks? How credible is NATO's program of reform aimed at alleviating the pressures of defense reductions?

6. How important is NATO to U.S. foreign policy? Does the "pivot" to the Asia-Pacific region mean a serious downgrading of U.S. strategic interest in Europe and NATO? What interests does the U.S. have in European security? How should these interests be prioritized relative to concerns about Asia, and China in particular?

7. Consider the 2011 NATO mission in Libya. Can European countries lead NATO? What would such leadership look like? Would it be welcomed by the U.S.? If Europe assumes greater leadership of NATO, would this shift result in a refocusing of NATO's priorities?

---

suggested readings

Hallams, Ellen and Schreer, Benjamin, "Towards a 'Post-American' Alliance? NATO Burden-sharing after Libya." **International Affairs** 88 (2012). 313–327. Available free online at: <http://www.chathamhouse.org/sites/default/files/public/International%20Affairs/2012/88_2/88_2hallamsschreer.pdf>. This article explores the meaning of a NATO in which the United States takes a lower profile and the related issue of how this might give rise to "a new transatlantic burden-sharing model."

Heisbourg, François, Wolfgang Ischinger, George Robertson, Kori Schake, and Valasek, Tomas, **All Alone? What US Retrenchment Means for Europe and NATO.** London, Centre for European Reform, 2012. Available free online at: <http://www.cer.org.uk/sites/default/files/publications/attachments/pdf/2012/rp_089_publish-4739.pdf>. In this article, a collection of high profile security analysts talk through the implications of American strategic reorientation for NATO and European security.

Ringsmose, Jens and Rynning, Sten (eds.), **NATO's New Strategic Concept: A Comprehensive Assessment.** Copenhagen, Danish Institute for International Studies, 2011. 196 pp. Available free online at: <http://www.diis.dk/graphics/Publications/Reports2011/RP2011-02-NATO_web.pdf>. This volume is framed by NATO's most recent keynote statement on strategy. It examines the meaning of that document as well as NATO's strategic environment and operational profile.

Rynning, Sten, "After Combat, the Perils of Partnership: NATO and Afghanistan beyond 2014." Research Paper. Rome, NATO Defense College, July 2012. Available free online at: <http://www.isn.ethz.ch/isn/Digital-Library/Publications/Detail/?lng=en&id=147777>. The most detailed discussion to date of NATO's role in Afghanistan in the coming years.

Shea, Jamie, "Keeping NATO Relevant." **Carnegie Endowment Policy Outlook**, April 2012. Available free online at: <http://carnegieendowment.org/2012/04/19/keeping-nato-relevant/acl9>. This article, written by one of the most astute and well-informed of NATO's officials, addresses how the alliance needs to reshape its efforts as it moves away from the preoccupation with Afghanistan.

Sloan, Stanley R., **Permanent Alliance? NATO and the Transatlantic Bargain from Truman to Obama**. New York, Continuum, 2010. 336 pp. $34.95 (paper). This book, written by one of the best-informed commentators on NATO, argues that the alliance rests on an enduring bargain between the United States and its allies, one that will ensure a continuing (if troubled existence) for NATO.

Sperling, James, and S. Victor Papacosma (eds.), **NATO after Sixty Years: A Stable Crisis.** Kent, Ohio, Kent State University Press, 2012. 328 pp. $65.00 (hardcover). This volume provides a comprehensive overview of NATO's current agenda and an exploration of the challenge of adaptation while tackling the issue of how the alliance can maintain its relevance in the twenty-first century.

Thies, Wallace J., **Why NATO Endures**. New York, Cambridge University Press, 2009. 334 pp. $105.00 (hardcover). Thies addresses the issue of "NATO in crisis" and argues that the self-healing properties of this alliance of democracies will ensure its future in the long term.

Myanmar and Southeast Asia
by Barbara Crossette

Supporters of Daw Aung San Suu Kyi, the leader of Myanmar's democracy movement, arrive for a campaign stop near Naypitaw, Myanmar, Mar. 5, 2012. They carry signs with her picture and that of her father, Aung San, founder of the Burmese army. (ADAM DEAN/THE NEW YORK TIMES/REDUX)

WHEN BURMA WON independence from Britain in 1948 it was a devastated country tormented by multiple crises. Geographical misfortune had placed this otherworldly Buddhist nation in the path of powerful armies in World War II as Japan battled Western allies for control of the strategically placed country. Its capital city, Rangoon, was heavily damaged; the old royal capital of Mandalay had been extensively destroyed by incendiary bombs. Oil wells and bridges had been taken out. Long-standing ethnic conflicts surfaced when peace returned, fracturing the nation from within. Aung San, the hero of Burmese independence and the great hope for national unity and renewal, was dead, assassinated at the age of 32 at the behest of a rival, barely six months before the modern country's birth.

And yet in spite of all this the nation still held great promise. It was rich in agricultural land and forests of teak and other hardwoods. There were still untapped oil and gas resources, and generous deposits of gemstones and minerals. Burma had been, and could have been again, a leading rice exporter to the world. Intellectual life was lively and cosmopolitan, and its universities in Mandalay and Rangoon were among Asia's best. Rangoon was a busy port and transportation hub for Southeast Asia, a bridge between East and West.

An important boon, from the Burmese nationalists' point of view, was the British decision in 1937 to separate Burma from Britain's larger Indian Empire, which then stretched from the borders of treacherous Afghanistan to the sultry lowlands and hills of what would become Bangladesh. The Burmese were thus guaranteed their own place on the map and were spared the possible fate of being swallowed up

BARBARA CROSSETTE, *a member of the Foreign Policy Association editorial board, is a former chief* New York Times *correspondent in Southeast Asia, South Asia and at the United Nations. In 2010 she won the Shorenstein Journalism Award for her writing on Asia, presented jointly by the Shorenstein Asia-Pacific Center at Stanford University, and the Shorenstein Center on Press, Politics, and Public Policy at Harvard University, part of the Kennedy School of Government.*

by their huge neighbor to the west after Indian independence in 1947.

By the late 1950's in Burma, there were signs of national revival under a constitutionally based democratic government and its prime minister, U Nu. But that brief era ended in 1962, when the military dictator General Ne Win seized power. Decades of repression and isolation under the Ne Win regime and its successors followed, as the country virtually closed its doors to the world, stifled national political activity and freedom of speech, took English out of the education system and public life and introduced madcap homegrown socialist economic policies that could have been written off as farce if they had not been so cruel in their effects on the country's people. Ne Win would dominate Burmese politics until the late

1980's, and the military would continue to rule directly until 2011.

Tumultuous events have marked the last two decades in Burma, renamed Myanmar by a military government in 1989 but still known widely as Burma, the name the democracy leader and Nobel Peace Prize winner Aung San Suu Kyi vows to keep. It is a country in uneasy balance between new democratic gains and a still-strong military lurking behind the scenes. As Myanmar now changes course and bids for a place in the international mainstream, would-be investors swarm its commercial and government centers, and tourists are returning in larger numbers. Aung San Suu Kyi, the leader of the political opposition and the daughter of the independence hero Aung San, won a seat in Parliament in 2012, leading her

National League for Democracy (NLD) into active political participation after years of persecution, severe jail terms for colleagues and student supporters, and at least one attempt, in 2003, to kill her as she toured the countryside during a spell of freedom amid long periods of house arrest.

The U.S. responded to the recent reforms by easing American sanctions. An experienced diplomat, Derek Mitchell, arrived in July as ambassador, the first full-fledged American ambassador assigned to the country in almost a quarter of a century. In November 2012, in a historic gesture to signal American support for the transition to democracy, Barack Obama became the first American president ever to make an official visit to the country.

The military's stunning decision to opt for wholesale transformation of this downtrodden and intellectually quarantined nation has been, without question, the most dramatic development in Southeast Asia in more than a decade, possibly a generation. As new policies are put in place, how this story will play out—or end—is a question that consumes the country's neighbors, international organizations and foreign governments, especially the U.S.

Who can help this nation recover? And how?

Political evolution, not yet a revolution

Ban Ki-moon, secretary-general of the United Nations and a former foreign minister of South Korea well-acquainted with Myanmar's tortured history, recalls that when he went to the country for the first time in his present capacity in 2008, he found a leadership that had backed itself into a corner. Cyclone Nargis had struck the Irrawaddy Delta with a wall of wind and water that left nearly 140,000 people dead and over two million displaced. The military government had shocked and infuriated the world when it barred all international emergency help, though this Asian disaster's toll was second only to that of the Indian Ocean tsunami of 2004.

Myanmar, considered a pariah by most democratic nations, had very few

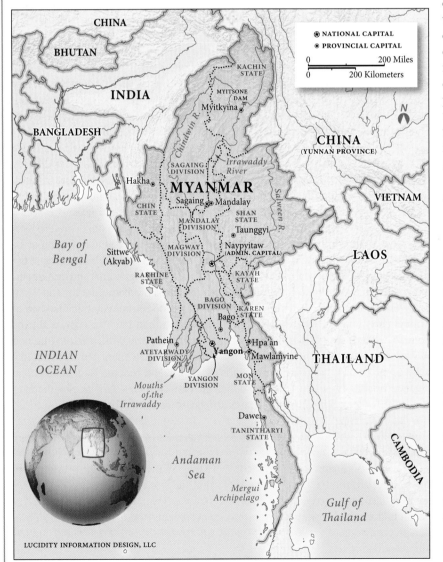

LUCIDITY INFORMATION DESIGN, LLC

Children walk through the devastation wrought by Cyclone Nargis in Myanmar, where most houses in this village south of Pyapon were destroyed. Many villages were hard to reach and aid was slow to arrive. (MARTIN SASSE/LAIF/REDUX)

UN Secretary General Ban Ki-Moon (center) makes a traditional gesture as he walks through a refugee camp on a tour to view conditions in cyclone damaged areas and to meet with Myanmar government officials. (STAN HONDA/AFP/POOL/GETTY IMAGES)

friends. One of them was North Korea, with which Myanmar had military and intelligence ties that included the sharing of some nuclear technology, to the distress of the U.S. and many other governments. In 1983, North Korean agents tried to assassinate the South Korean President Chun Doo Hwan, who was on an official visit in Rangoon. Chun survived, but 17 other South Korean officials died in the bombing. No South Korean government leader visited Myanmar again until 2012. India, concerned about Chinese influence, also maintained close ties with Myanmar, to the dismay of human rights organizations and the U.S., until the widespread persecution of democracy advocates in the late 1980's. Diplomatic relations between Myanmar and the U.S., as well as other nations, were at best minimal. International reporters, many based in neighboring Thailand, were only occasionally given visas to visit Myanmar. Correspondents often relied on reports from exile media, most notably *The Irrawaddy,* an online magazine published by exiled journalists in Thailand.

In 2008, after Cyclone Nargis had left people starving and drowning in ruined homes, the generals rejected or very sharply restricted aid from both international organizations and governments, and left food, shelter materials and technical help drifting on foreign ships off the coast, unable to land relief supplies. Bernard Kouchner, then the foreign minister of France, hinted at possible international intervention

under the doctrine of the "responsibility to protect" (R2P). David Cameron, then the leader of the British political opposition, called the decision to block aid "a crime against humanity." It was Ban's task to persuade the generals to reconsider this heartless response—and he had to negotiate his way into the country by promising not to discuss politics. Human rights monitors had been denied entry to the country for years, and development organizations had been restricted by both the generals' paranoia and stringent American sanctions. "It was very difficult because Myanmar was totally closed," Ban said in an interview at the United Nations in New York in August 2012. "They were very much afraid of foreign pressure." He said he told them: "Look, this is a totally unbearable tragedy for your country. You need to open up. You need to have some support from the international community. I'm not going to raise any political issues. I'm not going to ask for a meeting with Aung San Suu Kyi. I just want to meet the president and prime minister." The president at the time was Than Shwe, a tough and repressive general. His prime minister, Thein Sein, appeared to Ban to be a more flexible officer. Thein Sein is now Myanmar's reformist president.

After the leadership finally agreed to allow assistance to be funneled into the country through neighboring Thailand, Ban organized a donors' pledging conference in Yangon, as the military had renamed Rangoon. Donors were not

in a good mood. "The amount which we were able to mobilize was not that high," Ban said. "It was less than $100 million. In such circumstances that was very little. People were very angry." But it was, Ban said, "a good opening."

Events began to move quickly after that initial crack appeared in the wall of isolation. In 2009, Ban was invited back and gave an open public lecture attended by about 500 people, including students and government ministers, he said. He was roundly criticized by outsiders for making the trip at all. He answered his critics, many of them in Western governments and human rights organizations, by saying that he had to drive their message of openness home. Western nations had imposed crippling sanctions on the country, adding to its isolation, and many of the critics of the military regime wanted more punishment, not diplomacy.

"I needed to convey this message of pressure to General Than Shwe and the other military leadership there," he said in the interview. "If you really want the message of democratization directed to the ears of President Than Shwe, then I have to be there."

In 2010, the Than Shwe government called a national election, widely viewed as flawed. It was boycotted by Aung San Suu Kyi's NLD, the party that had won a national election in 1990 but was never permitted to govern. Not surprisingly, the 2010 election handed a decisive victory to the military-backed Union Solidarity and Development

Party (USDP). Nevertheless, the generals called the election a transition to democracy and, a week later, released Aung San Suu Kyi. She also got an Internet connection. Since then, press censorship has been lifted and the rules on peaceful public assembly have been relaxed. The names of thousands of foreigners and exiles barred from entering the country have been removed from a blacklist. The government has acknowledged publicly, moreover, that the NLD was indeed the clear winner of the 1990 vote.

Thein Sein, the former prime minister, resigned from the military and was sworn in as president in March 2011 as head of a nominally civilian government. Thousands of prisoners have been released since then and, although the Thailand-based Assistance Association of Political Prisoners-Burma still had several hundred names on its list at the end of 2012, Aung San Suu Kyi and the U.S. agree that the majority of detainees are now free, and many have resumed political activity.

In August 2011, in a step that has since proved to be a political watershed, President Thein Sein invited Aung San Suu Kyi to a meeting in the relatively new capital city of Naypyidaw, 205 miles north of the old capital, Rangoon. After some hesitation, Aung San Suu Kyi—whom the Burmese

Myanmar's pro-democracy leader Aung San Suu Kyi poses with President Thein Sein before their meeting in Myanmar's capital of Naypyitaw. Her father's portrait hangs in the background. (AP/CORBIS)

people refer to universally as simply The Lady—made the bold political decision to accept the invitation. People close to the event said that after a rather formal meeting in Thein Sein's office, the unlikely pair went to lunch in the presidential residence, where the atmosphere softened as Aung San Suu Kyi was greeted warmly by the president's wife, and could see a large portrait of Aung San, her father, prominently displayed. He was, after all, the founder of

the Burmese army. A year later, in July 2012, Thein Sein sent a vice president to join Aung San Suu Kyi in placing flowers on Aung San's tomb on the 65th anniversary of his death. The ceremony was reported by government media.

As for Aung San Suu Kyi—who in 2010 told Vijay Nambiar, the special representative of the United Nations secretary-general for Myanmar, that "a parody of democracy is infinitely worse than an outright dictatorship"—her views began to change after her meeting with the president, according to the envoy, an experienced former Indian diplomat who had earlier been Ban Ki-moon's chief of staff.

"The next time I met her," Nambiar said in an interview in August 2012, "she told me that she trusted him." But Nambiar also said that Aung San Suu Kyi made clear this trust did not extend to the military as a whole. "It's not as if she's changed her overall approach," he said. "Even today she carries a very strong sense of skepticism if not outright disbelief about these changes that are taking place. But she's decided to work with it and try to open more and more doors."

Aung San Suu Kyi was also aware that among democracy advocates there was an uneasy feeling that an indefinite political boycott could marginalize them and be self-defeating. Nambiar said that through decades of tension and uncertainty, "things were difficult for civil society organizations, but there were a few which had managed in those difficult times to carve out a little space for themselves. They said it would be a pity if they were to lose completely even the little bit of space we've got now."

When by-elections for the national Parliament were scheduled for April 2012, Aung San Suu Kyi and the NLD decided to take part. Around the country, 45 seats in the 664-seat bicameral legislature were to be filled. The NLD won 43 of the 44 it contested, taking 66 percent of the national vote in a landslide finish. Domestic and foreign poll observers concluded that the voting had been generally free and fair.

In Yangon now, the makeshift offices of other, nascent political parties

Aung San Suu Kyi greets supporters during a campaign stop in Naypitaw, Myanmar, on March 5, 2012. (ADAM DEAN/THE NEW YORK TIMES/REDUX)

and advocacy groups are humming with activity as they look ahead to important national elections in 2015. Former prisoners who had been arrested in a roundup of students and other dissidents in 1988—calling themselves "the 88ers"—have formed civic action groups. Eager young journalists jam their news conferences, sometimes sitting cramped on floors in stifling rooms where air-conditioning is an unheard of luxury. Tropical Myanmar is disastrously short of energy.

The NLD still accounts for less than seven percent of the seats in Parliament, with the military holding 25 percent—reserved for them and filled by appointment—and the military-backed USDP most of the rest, with some seats set aside for ethnic minorities. But if numbers are small, the symbolism is great.

Myanmar now has a bona fide, credible political opposition for the first time in 50 years. ∎

A fractured country in search of unity

FOR CENTURIES, what became known as the nation of Burma was battered not only by periods of disunity and civil war among numerous small kingdoms and ethnic clans but also by foreign invasions, including a Mongol attack by Kublai Khan that captured the temple city of Pagan. In the 19th century, the British took over the country step by step, culminating in 1885 with the capture of Mandalay, the royal capital, and with it the Court of Ava, Burma's last kingdom.

In his evocative personal journey through the Burmese past, *The River of Lost Footsteps: Histories of Burma,* Thant Myint-U, arguably the country's leading writer in English (and the grandson of U Thant, the only Asian United Nations secretary-general before Ban Ki-moon) describes the arrival of Brigadier George Stuart White, the British officer who sailed up the Irrawaddy to Mandalay aboard the steamship *Kathleen* to take the surrender of King Thibaw.

"By late November, the weather in Upper Burma is nearly always perfect, with cool nights and warm days of cloudless blue skies," Thant Myint-U wrote. "Brigadier White, standing on the deck as the *Kathleen* came within sight of Ava, wrote that 'the sun was pouring a flood of golden light on the last hours of Burman independence.'"

Ethnic divisions and armed rebellions did not begin or end with British rule. Many Burmese blamed the British for favoring one ethnic group, the Karen, strengthening their resolve and adding to the resentment of others.

When Aung San, an ethnic Burman, returned from successful negotiations with the British in January 1947 as head of a transitional government and with the promise of independence within a year, dangerous minority disaffections were high on his list of priorities. He also faced political challenges from Communists who sought to steer away from close ties with Western capitalist nations.

Ethnically, Burmans are the country's largest group, with about 68 percent of the population. The Shan people of the northeast comprise another 9 percent; the Karen in the southeast, 7 percent; the Rakhine (also known as Arakanese) on the Bay of Bengal, 4 percent; ethnic Chinese, 3 percent; Mon, 2 percent; and other smaller but important communities such as the Chin, Kachin, Karenni and Wa account for the rest. In all, there are thought to be more than 100 ethnic groups, many of them territorial and rooted deeply in local populations with their own languages.

Aung San set out to reach agreements with ethnic minorities at a conference in 1947 in the Shan state, a project called Panglong I, named after the site of the meetings. Current leaders, including Aung San Suu Kyi and some government officials, are talking about convening a Panglong II to pick up where the assassination of Aung San and the military's rejection of the reconciliation process left off. Until early in this century, the Burmese—and, significantly, Burman—army and government opted for a military solution to ethnic rebellions. The army's campaigns have been marked by internationally condemned human rights abuses, the further alienation of minorities and the flight of

Female recruits of the Kachin Independent Army (KIA), do early morning training with fake wooden rifles in a military camp in May 2012. Fighting between the Burmese army and the KIA continues in 2012. (Q. SAKAMAKI/REDUX)

Rescue workers clear debris from destroyed houses following days of sectarian violence in Sittwe, the capital of Myanmar's western state of Rakhine, on June 16, 2012. The UN warned of "immense hardship" faced by thousands displaced by rioting. (AFP/GETTY IMAGES)

many people into Thailand, China and the West.

The Panglong I agreement, designed by Aung San to be widely appealing, promised ethnic states considerable autonomy within the Burmese union and the right to leave it after 10 years if the people wanted out. The writer Thant Myint-U (now a presidential adviser) called Burma "the only British possession to gain independence with the option for a future breakup built into the constitution."

Military attempts to quell ethnic discontents go on. Human Rights Watch in its *World Report 2012* said that fighting had actually spread in 2011, in particular with the Kachin Independence Army, and continued through 2012. Tens of thousands of civilians have been reported displaced in recent battles with the military, which has not lost its reputation for brutality.

"The Burmese military continues to violate international humanitarian law through the use of anti-personnel landmines, extrajudicial killings, forced labor, torture, beatings, and pillaging of property," Human Rights Watch said. "Sexual violence against women and girls remains a serious problem and perpetrators are rarely brought to justice. The army continues to actively recruit and use child soldiers." In September 2012, the government said that child soldiers were being identified

and would be freed. The first to be discharged were reunited with their families to great fanfare.

Religion has not been a major factor in most of Myanmar's separatist movements, though a few ethnic groups have large Christian populations. An exception has been the Rakhine (formerly Arakan) state, where Muslims and Buddhists have clashed in deadly confrontations over the past year. Myanmar was for many centuries, and still is, an overwhelmingly Theravada Buddhist nation, a school of Buddhism also practiced in Thailand, Laos and Sri Lanka. Burmese monks have been a strong presence in political life, risking death, beatings and imprisonment to oppose the military and support democracy. Buddhist monks, however, can also be nationalistic, even violent, in defense of their religion and culture, which they see as defining the nation-state—a phenomenon also seen in Buddhist-majority Sri Lanka's long civil war with Tamil insurgents.

When long-simmering tensions boiled over into violence in 2012 in Rakhine/Arakan state, Muslims known as Rohingyas were attacked after reports spread that a Buddhist woman had been raped and killed. According to local reports, Buddhists had fueled the violence with the revenge murder of 10 Rohingyas. Scores of people were killed. Yet many Burmese politicians pulled back from condemnation of Buddhists be-

cause of the political influence of the monks, experts say. When local employees of United Nations relief agencies tried to help, three were arrested. They were pardoned several months later by the president.

The full story of the extremely violent confrontations is the subject of another Human Rights Watch report, *The Government Could Have Stopped This: Sectarian Violence and Ensuing Abuses in Burma's Arakan State*. In response to an international outcry, the government established a commission to investigate the violence and has opened the region to inspection by outsiders, including American diplomats and a delegation from the Organization of Islamic Cooperation.

Rakhine/Arakan state has two groups of Muslims, one whose families trace their ancestry to years before 1824, when the British took over the region and annexed it to India, and a second and much larger group whose families migrated from what is now Bangladesh (originally part of the British Indian state of Bengal) after 1824. Since independence in 1948, the Burmese government has denied the latter group citizenship, continuing to see them as a refugee population that has no place in Burmese, particularly Burman Buddhist, society. Bangladesh, though populated by fellow Muslim Bengalis, will not admit them. "There are almost a million people who are stateless," Nambiar said. "Even Daw Aung San Suu Kyi finds that she cannot come out very strongly on this," he said. "She talks of having laws which are in keeping with international human rights standards, but not beyond that." In Washington in September 2012, Aung San Suu Kyi stuck to that position, not offering any immediate promises to the Rohingyas. By the end of the year, however, she was calling for military intervention, according to *The Irrawaddy*. The military, however, is dominated by Burman Buddhists.

Josef Silverstein, professor emeritus at Rutgers University and a lifelong scholar of Myanmar who early in his career studied and later lectured at Mandalay University, said in an interview that the lack of national unity is the biggest question hanging over the country's future.

"This is not a homogenous society," he said. "Although we think of it as a Buddhist country, and we think of the Burmese as the dominant people in it, nevertheless there are pockets in the border regions, particularly down the western frontier, which share both land and sea between the peoples of Burma and the peoples of the Indian subcontinent. On the east side, particularly in the northeast, where the Shan and the Karen and others have lived for so long and have fought off or resisted integration and acceptance, you see that the country has been in tension for as long as people have been keeping records."

The government has only recently formed a peace commission to reopen the issue of national reconciliation, but the creation of a federal system of state governments for ethnic regions is not seen as politically possible. "As long as the government refuses to adopt the principles of equality amongst all people, and treats different ones in different ways, you do not have people thinking of themselves as part of the country," Silverstein said. "People must be able to say, Yes, I'm a Burmese; I am also a Muslim; I am also this, that or the other," he said. The primacy of national identity is the "absent glue" needed to hold Burma together and prevent repeated upheavals, he said.

Thein Sein's ambitious agenda

Thein Sein, who was elected president by the military-dominated Parliament, not in a popular vote, had been in office for about 15 months when he gave a major address in June 2012 to officials from national, state and local levels of government—a kind of "state of the union" pep talk. He started with a self-congratulatory summation of his accomplishments and then turned to the economy and national development. His goals soared, but his own assessment of what needed to be done to reach them was sobering. By 2016, he said, his government projected a 7.7 percent annual increase in gross national prod-

Instead of modern skyscrapers one sees worn-down buildings in Myanmar's capital city of Yangon, March 2011. (JUSTIN MOTT/REDUX)

uct (GNP) and a 1.7 percent rise in per capita gross domestic product (GDP). Against this, he acknowledged, were the drag factors of limited government funds; the need for more aid, grants and loans from abroad; and the need for increased investment, both domestic and foreign.

Important, the president said, was shrinking the government's role in the economy and encouraging privatization, starting with communications, energy, forestry, health and financial sectors. He acknowledged that opening the economy and framing development plans down to the township and village level will require the help of nongovernmental experts as well as international organizations. The United Nations Population Fund, for example, will help with a national census, collecting the data crucial in development planning.

The president said that ministries will be expected to review and reform their fiscal operations, with an emphasis on spending with a bottom-up rather than top-down approach to development. A minimum wage will be established and environmental protection introduced in project planning. Special economic zones will be created. Trade laws and practices are being aligned with international norms, he said. The list went on and on.

Jason Szep, in one of a series of excellent special reports on Myanmar for Reuters in 2012, wrote that

the government "is pushing ahead so fast that foreign advisers here on the ground say it risks overloading its rickety institutions."

The leadership hopes to lure back exiles who possess skills gained studying and working in more-developed countries. Some of them are returning on exploratory trips. Some decide to come back to stay, but many conclude sadly that there is still little immediate hope of finding jobs or creating new companies in fields such as information technology or new energy systems—sectors where the country desperately needs their skills—until legal protections and clearer investment codes are in place. Reacting to foot-dragging from within his government, Thein Sein has dismissed ministers and other officials considered hard-liners standing in the way of reforms.

Aung San Suu Kyi caused a stir when she warned in remarks at a World Economic Forum session in Thailand in the spring of 2012 against "reckless optimism" among investors. Nambiar, the United Nations envoy, agrees. "People are now going to put a lot of money in, but how much of it can Myanmar absorb?" he asked, pointing to situations in other countries where a sudden influx of uncoordinated aid led to extra costs, crippling corruption, competition among donors, bureaucratic hurdles and quarrels with local people over priorities.

Furthermore, a sudden influx of aid and investment money—and the foreigners who come with it—often leads to catastrophic increases in property prices and rents, and families see living costs rise while wages stagnate. In Yangon, new luxury tourist hotels, condominiums, serviced apartment blocks and garishly ostentatious mansions are already rising over genteel avenues shaded by old trees. Some magnificent, if decrepit, examples of colonial-era (but uniquely Burmese-inspired) architecture are threatened by demolition. At this writing, a group of lawyers is organizing to try to save an historic courthouse that a Chinese developer plans to raze and replace with a hotel.

In his reporting in Myanmar, Szep found government ministries "inexperienced and thinly staffed" while taking on huge workloads and trying to learn on the job. The government knows there is a problem created by decades of isolation from the global economy. Szep quoted a vice president saying that applicants for government positions may soon face tests of their skills and qualifications, an indication that this is something novel.

One long-term uncertainty surrounds how the government will deal with property rights, particularly on agricul-

tural land, which is the key to restoring a stronger export trade in that sector as well as the confidence of rural people. There are some ominous signs of trouble ahead. A new agriculture policy suggests consolidating small farms into plantation-sized agribusinesses for the sake of "efficiency." Land seizures for large-scale food production and other industries have provoked organized resistance. Recently in the Sagaing region in the northwest, thousands have joined protests over plans to give farmland to an expanding Chinese-run copper mine. Outside of urban areas, the government owns virtually all the land, and the military has enjoyed a free hand in dictating its use for its own financial interests.

"Remember we're talking about basically an agricultural country," said Silverstein, the historian. "It is not an industrial state. The economy is dominated by the military, who have taken the land from the people and distributed it amongst themselves or put themselves in management positions to benefit from whatever success happens there. So the first change has to begin around the question of property," he said. "Can an individual pass that property on to his family? Can a person buy and sell property? Unless there is a rule that applies to everybody, and the courts—if they ever get them functioning properly—will honor that rule, I don't think there's any way for Burma to come together." An irreparably corrupted judicial system leaves no legal recourse for the dispossessed. "As a result, in a country that is rich in natural resources, people are not going to do more than try to harvest what little they have and sell the surplus or hide the evidence so they have enough to feed their families," he said.

Myanmar is poor, with the lowest annual per capita income in Southeast Asia, at $1,950, close to Cambodia's $2,080, but roughly half that of the Philippines ($3,980) and less than a quarter of Thailand's $8,190, according to the 2012 World Population Data Sheet from the Population Reference Bureau, a nongovernmental research organization in Washington, D.C.

Life expectancy for the country's 55

million to 60 million people (estimates vary) is 65 years of age, low for a region where the average stands at 71. Its infant mortality rate, at 51 deaths for every 1,000 live births, is almost double the regional average. Maternal mortality is above Southeast Asian levels.

Yet the population has a high literacy rate of 92 percent, according to the World Bank and United Nations agencies. This would indicate a strong interest in education, fostered by families who often rely on simple schools run by Buddhist monks and nuns.

In one of Yangon's poorest neighborhoods, a 70-year-old monk who opened a school for boys (and a few girls) 20 years ago demonstrates how monasteries have become alternative centers for both education and health services. The monk, U Margainda, and his monastic community educate and care for about 100 resident children, providing not only schooling and room and board but also health care, all paid for by donations from domestic and foreign Buddhists, many from Thailand, Vietnam and Japan, as well as from various other donors. Volunteer doctors from European nongovernmental organizations (NGOs) run a German-built clinic in the monastery compound that is well enough equipped for simple surgical procedures.

"We teach them their letters and numbers and tell them stories," U Margainda said of his pupils, poor children whose parents have brought them to the monastery because they cannot feed them or meet the hidden costs of even "free" public schools. The children can remain in the monastery to high school level, but even if they leave early, as most do, they can achieve reasonably good basic literacy and mathematical knowledge. This pattern of monastery education is found to one degree or another, depending on local resources, across the country. The parallel education system, rare in a nation so poor, has hopefully created a trainable youthful population ready to fill jobs as development progresses. Universal education and high literacy rates in East Asia and Southeast Asia played a central role in the creation of "tiger" economies. ■

The neighborhood and the world

MYANMAR, a mainland Southeast Asian country slightly smaller than Texas (or a little larger than France), borders Thailand, Laos, China, India and Bangladesh. Its ocean coastlines are in the southwest, on the Andaman Sea and the Bay of Bengal, facing South Asia. To the east, the country is more closely aligned politically and culturally across land borders with Southeast Asian neighbors, especially Thailand.

Myanmar joined the Association of Southeast Asian Nations, known as ASEAN, in 1997. The decision by ASEAN's then nine member states — Brunei, Cambodia, Indonesia, Laos, Malaysia, the Philippines, Singapore, Thailand and Vietnam — to welcome Myanmar into a regional organization whose nations are theoretically civilian-led, with popular representation and free-enterprise economies, was controversial internationally. Myanmar obviously met none of those qualifications.

"For 15 years since joining ASEAN, Burma was considered an albatross around ASEAN's neck until the rapid transformation began," Kavi Chongkittavorn, a leading Thai journalist wrote in *The Nation* newspaper in Bangkok in February 2012. Myanmar may not have been the only questionable candidate for ASEAN over the years. Laos, Cambodia and Vietnam were and still are essentially one-party states. Singapore had a token opposition, Indonesia was ruled for decades by a general in civilian clothes and Thailand's army has been a force in politics for generations.

But the generals were of a different order altogether. Now their political reforms, and the more open attitude of President Thein Sein, have eased some of the awkwardness about their place in the organization. ASEAN, which recently celebrated its 45th anniversary, has taken a gamble on allowing Myanmar to hold the chairmanship of the organization for 2014. Around the region and beyond there are questions about whether the government and bureaucratic machinery can meet the challenges of the task.

Nambiar, the United Nations special representative, said that "ASEAN has placed a lot of expectations on Myanmar," especially given that its chairmanship year will lead up to the formal establishment in 2015 of the ASEAN Economic Community (an echo of the early 27-member European Union [EU] and other regional groupings). "Myanmar will have to polish up its act," Nambiar said. "It will have to rise to the full level of leadership."

That will entail staging important conferences and other events that will tax its corps of officials who are inexperienced with dealing with intergovernmental issues and practices. An early test will come in 2013, when Myanmar will be host to a major regional sports event, the Southeast Asia (SEA) Games. On the diplomatic front, ASEAN has regular meetings with nonmember partner nations such as the U.S., Japan, China, Australia and the EU. "No doubt, Burma has a lot of catching up to do," the Thai analyst and journalist Kavi Chongkit-tavorn wrote in *The Nation*. "Burma must integrate with ASEAN and tap into the grouping's dynamism and abundant resources."

Beyond ASEAN, no nations have as much interest in expanding in Myanmar as China and India, two of the three largest importers of the country's commodities, including natural gas, timber products and gemstones. Thailand, which takes about 37 percent of Myanmar's exports, ranks first, China second with 19 percent and India third at 12.3 percent, according to U.S. calculations. But import and export figures are only part of the motivation for China and India to expand their influence in Myanmar, which both see as strategic. China has for many years sought an overland route to open water that bypasses the crowded and pirate-prone Straits of Malacca. India fears that direct Chinese access to the sea in the Bay of Bengal could pose a security threat.

As India prepares for national elections in 2014, it has been bogged down in economic and political crises at the national level, on top of renewed armed unrest in the seven states of the remote Indian Northeast bordering Myanmar (and ongoing separatism in Kashmir as well as a Maoist guerrilla war in the interior of the country). But India still has big hopes of increasing its presence in Myanmar, diplomatically and commercially, after decades of leaving its options

Leaders from the Association of Southeast Asian Nations (ASEAN) hold hands for a group photo during the opening ceremony of the 20th ASEAN Summit in Phnom Penh, Cambodia, April 3, 2012. From left, Brunei's Sultan Hassanal Bolkiah, Indonesia's Vice President Boediono, Laos' Prime Minister Thongsing Thammavong, Malaysia's Prime Minister Najib Razak and Myanmar President Thein Sein. (AP/APICHART WEERAWONG/CORBIS)

Laurent Gbagbo (c.), Côte d'Ivoire's former president, at the International Criminal Court in The Hague, Netherlands, on December 5, 2011. Gbagbo, who was arrested the previous week in the Côte d'Ivoire, is facing charges of crimes against humanity, including murder and rape, following violence in the country's 2010 presidential elections. (PETER DE JONG/POOL/THE NEW YORK TIMES/REDUX)

For three months and in a fashion far more typical than its pace in Libya, the Security Council dragged its collective feet. The result was predictable: refugees, massacres, full-scale civil war and a ruined economy. In the aftermath of robust action against Libya, on March 30 the council authorized UNOCI in UNSCR 1975 to "use all necessary means" to implement its mandate in protecting civilians and in self-defense.

That decision was the third time in March 2011 alone that the Security Council had menaced the loser of the elections. The empty resolution-rattling ended early in April. Driven more by French domestic politics than R2P, Paris approved robust military action by its 1,650-strong Licorne contingent as the avant-garde of the UNOCI. The unwillingness to apply armed force had abetted Gbagbo's intransigence and resulted in the country's train wreck. As heavy fighting broke out between the opposing factions, the United Nations operation finally attacked pro-Gbagbo military installations. Ultimately, the violence was ended by Outtara's troops who, with French assistance, assaulted Gbagbo's residence and arrested the former president.

Posing counter-factual questions is invariably unsatisfying, but answers to the following two seem clear: Was it necessary to enable war crimes and crimes against humanity, a million refugees and a ravaged economy? Although Gbagbo was indicted by the International Criminal Court (ICC) where he appeared in December 2011, should he have been inscribed on the ICC's docket earlier and put in custody in The Hague?

Answers to the following are less obvious: Was the United Nations' presence an impediment to more robust and timely action by ECOWAS and the AU? Was the resort to enforcement action by the ex-colonial power helpful or hurtful to R2P's normative advance?

The "why" for international action in Côte d'Ivoire was also that it was justifiable and doable even if it took longer than it should have; even so, the benefits outweighed the costs for the intervening and neighboring countries.

Washington had no dog in this fight, but its diplomatic engagement with regional and international partners unleashed French ground troops in combination with the modest peacekeeping contingent, which ended the violent electoral standoff and protected civilians.   ■

Why not Syria?

THERE HAS HARDLY been too much but rather too little humanitarian intervention. Accusations of Western imperialism provide a predictable distraction in spite of support across the global South favoring robust humanitarian intervention. For example, the Arab League, GCC and AU supported outside intervention in Libya and ECOWAS supported it throughout the crisis in Côte d'Ivoire. "Though some critics fret that R2P could prove to be a humanitarian veneer by which powerful states could justify military intervention in the development world, more often the problem has been the opposite," Edward Luck tells us. "The capable have stood by as the slaughter of civilians unfolded before the world's—and sometimes even UN peacekeepers'—eyes. They have looked for excuses not to act, rather than for reasons to intervene."

That certainly summarizes how states have remained on the sidelines while vigorously condemning Syria's bloodbath and watching successive agreements go up in flames. Fifteen children scribbled "the people want the regime to fall" on a wall in the southern city of Dara'a and stirred a massive popular protest. The graffiti unleashed Assad's brutal repression in March 2011. It took until August for the Security Council to issue merely a condemnatory presidential statement. Thereafter, the threat of an actual double veto by China and Russia paralyzed the council.

The anemic international response to Syria's plight has confirmed that United Nations members are more able than in the past to condemn abhorrent conduct but often remain unable to agree on a common course of action even in the face of mass atrocities. The first year alone of Assad's murderous repression resulted in some 12,000 victims, which finally led the Arab League and United Nations to appoint a joint envoy, Kofi Annan.

The first two points of what turned out to be his dead-on-arrival six-point plan were a cease-fire and humanitarian access; and the Security Council approved sending some 300 unarmed monitors to replace a handful of ineffective Arab League ones. As the violence was mainly a government affair at that time, the call for a cease-fire and humanitarian access seemed especially hollow when over 100 civilians (almost half of whom were children) were killed in the massacre in Houla in late spring, which led a host of Western countries to pull their ambassadors and the United Nations to suspend the monitoring mission. Futile diplomatic dances took place in Moscow and Geneva as fatalities mounted. Fed up with his "mission impossible," in August 2012 Annan resigned and concluded an op-ed in the *Financial Times*: "President Bashar al-Assad must leave office." The Security Council saw no point in renewing the mandate of the observers but approved a replacement envoy, the former Algerian foreign minister and longtime troubleshooter, Lakhdar Brahimi.

Syria demonstrates, if there was any doubt, that a robust R2P response is never automatic. Widespread diplomatic and public lamentations were audible while government security forces deployed tanks, warships and heavy weapons against civilians. In addition to the politics in the Security Council, Syria also confounded easy generalizations and looked distinctly more complicated, chancy and confused than Libya. Whereas the latter's relatively cohesive opposition movement was run from inside and spoke with one voice, the former's was based outside as well as inside the country, dispersed geographically and divided politically. The visible but fractious central opposition group in exile, the Syrian National Council, was divided among the Muslim Brotherhood (itself split into more and less tolerant factions) and two other Islamist organizations, the National Action Group and the Syria

Syrian President Bashar al-Assad waves at supporters during a rare public appearance in Damascus on January 11, 2012 in which he vowed to defeat a "conspiracy" against Syria, a day after he blamed foreign interests for stoking months of deadly violence. (AFP/ GETTY IMAGES)

National Movement. Indeed, an attempt to cobble together a more unified opposition—in Cairo in June—ended in acrimony and failure.

Within the country's borders, about 100 ragtag groups of fighters and unarmed protesters agreed on little except that Assad must go. Inchoate and unable to coalesce into a unified force, they had no common ideology; and they lacked a clear chain of command to coordinate operations, protests or arms supplies. It was not until September 2012, in fact, that the main force, the Free Syrian Army, moved its headquarters from Turkey. Whereas three quarters of the Libyan population lived in areas that broke away from the regime and fell quickly under rebel control, in Syria the opposition has been unable to maintain control over major population concentrations. In fact, the opposition also has been incapable of exerting control over fighters who, increasingly, have committed crimes similar to those of the regime.

Moreover, instead of virtually an entire country (excepting those on his payroll) being mobilized against Qaddafi, a substantial number of Syrians support the regime or are on the sidelines waiting to see who will end up on top. The Assad government appears to have

sufficient firepower and support among minorities to keep fighting. In contrast to Libya's virtually homogenous population (Arabized Berbers, nearly all Sunni Muslims), Syria's diversity is striking. Arabs constitute 90 percent of the population, but there are substantial numbers of Kurds, Armenians and others. In terms of religion, Sunni Muslims are about three quarters of the population, and another 15 percent are Alawites (an offshoot of Shiite Islam), Druze and other Muslim sects; and in addition to possible inter-Muslim divides, there is a possible cleavage with the Christian 10 percent of the population. Unlike Libya's largely desert-like terrain with a few isolated cities, Syria's numerous urban areas mean that surgical airstrikes are implausible and that significant civilian deaths from military action are guaranteed. Rather than Libya's small mercenary army that quickly defected or departed, the Syrian armed forces for the most part remain well equipped, disciplined and loyal.

An additional complication arose in September 2012 with the protests across the Middle East and elsewhere that erupted after a shoddy 14-minute video lampooning the Prophet Muhammad went viral. There is no guarantee against the incendiary power of anti-

American rage and Islamist sentiments, which Assad had kept in check over the years.

As Western and certainly U.S. boots on the ground were never possibilities, the main coercive options were to create safe havens on Syria's borders (suggested by Princeton professor Anne-Marie Slaughter) or to arm the opposition (suggested by Senator John McCain, R–Ariz.). Neither received much support outside of op-ed pages although the administration provided communications equipment and training, shared intelligence and formed a task force with Turkey for a post-Assad Syria. The former option would have required cooperation among six neighbors with their own quarrels (Israel, Lebanon, Jordan, Iraq, Iran and Turkey) and the latter undoubtedly would have quickly led to an even bloodier civil war. These neighbors have not been as bashful, however, with Turkey furnishing arms and Saudia Arabia and Qatar providing funds to purchase them. Meanwhile, Moscow continued to supply all manner of weapons to the Assad regime, which also had support from Iran as well as Shiite fighters from Iraq, Lebanon and Iran. All borders are arbitrary but Syria's especially so; all of its communities are linked to brethren in neighboring countries and seek to draw them into the armed conflict.

The civil war grinds on, gradually taking on the character of a sectarian regional battleground. The government and the opposition both believe that they can fight their way to victory, but neither seemingly has the capacity to do more than win minor tactical victories. Brahimi gave his bleak initial appraisal to the Security Council in September and announced a cease-fire in October for Id al-Adha, the Muslim feast of sacrifice. Like the previous one negotiated in April by his predecessor, the October version fell apart almost immediately and failed to slow the tempo of killing.

Opposition consolidation

However, with their eye on increased money and military aid, opposition negotiators agreed after several days of haggling in Qatar in November to form the National Coalition of Syrian Revolutionary and Opposition Forces, which elected as its president Sheikh Ahmad Moaz al-Khatib, a former imam of the historic Umayyad mosque in Damascus. Under heavy pressure from outsiders—and especially Washington, where Secretary of State Hillary Clinton wanted such a consolidation before leaving office—the new umbrella organization subsumed the Syrian National Council, a previous attempt at unification that was increasingly marginalized

and fragmented as Syria descended into full-blown civil war. The expectation was that the new coalition would assume Syria's seat in the Arab League and that countries would recognize it. France immediately recognized the coalition, replicating perhaps the same dynamic that began with the recognition of the Libyan rebels who eventually toppled Qaddafi. Whether the newly coalesced group can hold together remains uncertain.

Sustained stalemate and slaughter thus seem likely unless all sides can agree on a post-Assad, power-sharing agreement. Such an arrangement would require a negotiated exit for Assad that could be supported by the West, Russia, China and Iran. Given the accounts to be settled, no such agreement would be credible without foreign soldiers (perhaps deployed by the United Nations and the Arab League). Atrocities are widespread, but the overwhelming balance tips toward the regime; Assad and his generals eventually have to find their way on to The Hague's docket.

The responsibility to protect is a principle and not a tactic, and the principle remained intact in Syria even if international action was considerably less fulsome than in Libya or even in Côte d'Ivoire. "When governments turn to mass murder, we may have no easy solutions," *New York Times* columnist Nicholas D. Kristof counsels, "but we should at least be crystal clear about which side we're on." In fact, the transformation of international attitudes is remarkable if one contrasts the deafening silence that greeted the 1982 massacre by Hafez al-Assad of some 40,000 people in an artillery barrage of Hama with the steady stream of hostile condemnations of his son's machinations: the United Nations' Joint Office on the Prevention of Genocide and R2P called for a halt to crimes against humanity; the Human Rights Council condemned the crimes by a crushing vote and published a report detailing extensive crimes; the U.S., the EU and other states imposed sanctions; the Arab League condemned the actions, formulated

Syrian president Bashar al-Assad (r.) meets with UN-Arab League special envoy to Syria, Kofi Annan, in Damascus, Syria, July 9, 2012. Annan was unsuccessful in brokering and end to the current violence in Syria. (SNA/XINHUA/CORBIS)

a peace plan and sent human rights monitors; and the General Assembly initially condemned the violence and supported the peace plan with a two-thirds majority and on two subsequent occasions even more overwhelmingly (only 12 of 193 states voted against the resolutions) condemned Assad's unbridled crackdown and mass atrocities and specifically called for his resignation. While of little solace to Syria's victims and their families, these calls reaffirmed the R2P principle. In comparison with Libya, the "why not" for Washington and for other major powers was that the politics in Syria and at the United Nations were totally different as well as the geography and the demography; moreover, the potential costs appeared to outweigh the benefits of coercion. ∎

The Atrocity Prevention Board and policy options

USUALLY NORMS have more clout once they are embedded in institutional structures with resources and personnel. For example, establishing a joint office by the United Nations and the appointment of "focal points" (senior-level officials who promote R2P at the national level) by almost 20 countries (with another 10 slated to do so) were steps in the right direction to internalize R2P.

Perhaps the most significant new structure resulted from Presidential Study Directive-10. This initiative and the decision to act in Libya emanated from the "dream team" of genocide prevention consisting of Secretary Clinton, U.S. Ambassador to the United Nations Susan Rice and Special Assistant to the President Samantha Power. In August 2011, President Obama established the Atrocity Prevention Board (APB)—an interagency mechanism to facilitate rapid reaction across the U.S. government and prevent mass atrocities. "Our security is affected when masses of civilians are slaughtered, refugees flow across borders and murderers wreak havoc on regional stability and livelihoods," he stated when unveiling the idea. "America's reputation suffers and our ability to bring about change is constrained, when we are perceived as idle in the face of mass atrocities and genocide."

The APB gathered for the first time at the White House on April 23, 2012, co-inciding with the annual remembrance of the Holocaust. Sixty-seven years after the end of that tragedy and 18 after the beginning of Rwanda's nightmare, the president announced that the U.S.

A French soldier is greeted by Tutsi children June 24, 1994, at the Nyarushishi Tutsi refugee camp in Gisenyi, Rwanda. The French military is visiting the camp to demonstrate France's neutral and humanitarian intentions during Operation Turquoise, despite French support for the Hutu government. (SCOTT PETERSON/LIAISON/GETTY)

would produce a National Intelligence Estimate for potential mass atrocities worldwide. Obama reiterated his administration's efforts at "institutionalizing" how the government mobilizes to prevent and halt mass atrocities. The White House highlighted a strategy in which the prevention of atrocities was not only a moral responsibility but a core national security interest as well. Organizations are not the answers to all our prayers, but they provide a bureaucratic means to enhance accountability. For instance, the APB's monthly meetings provide a means to hold senior officials' feet to the fire for keeping on top of volatile situations, and training programs expose younger foreign service officers to the idea that protecting civilians is an integral part of their job descriptions.

In thinking about future policy options, it would be foolish for the APB or any other body to overlook or discount five risks of deploying military force for human protection purposes. First, it may be premature and not give such other coercive but nonforcible measures as sanctions the chance to work. Second, military force may do more harm than good, and the unintended and intended consequences (sometimes euphemistically labeled "collateral damage") may outweigh the actual benefits of deploying military assets. Third, those applying force may exceed the terms of an approved mandate; the dispute over the extent of NATO action in Libya is one illustration, but another is blowback (in the aftermath of dead soldiers in Somalia in 1993, for instance) that may compromise future decisions about preventing or halting mass atrocities (in Rwanda in 1994, for instance). Fourth, military force may fail if an operation is done poorly or assets deployed inadequately and such a failure may thereby threaten R2P's future application. Finally, the unpredictable aftermath of military force and the inevitable difficulties of post-conflict peace-building may also color the perception of the norm.

Risks of inaction

These criticisms have all been levied in the aftermath of Libya, but inaction carries its own risks as well. It would be shortsighted to ignore risks from *not* using military force when mass atrocities threaten. First and foremost, catastrophic suffering could occur of exactly the type that since the Holocaust the international community has continually pledged to permit "never again." Second, states would once again shame themselves and make a mockery of international law by looking the other way in the face of mass murder. Third, if coercive force is postponed and displacement and revenge killings mount, options are reduced and the potential costs of deploying military assets could preclude action. Fourth, collective spinelessness could send the wrong message to other would-be thugs, thereby weakening the deterrent effects of future international diplomacy.

No task is more fraught than a decision to deploy military force. For humanitarian intervention, the main policy options follow from answers to the following questions:

Has there been movement beyond the "Somalia syndrome" and the apparent necessity for "near zero" casualties for U.S. soldiers coming to the rescue, no matter how many victims are saved?

Have prudent considerations been given their due and are the imagined benefits of averted atrocities (which involve counter-factual speculation) persuasive enough to outweigh the visible and certain destructiveness of a humanitarian intervention?

Does an exit strategy address "mis-

sion creep" because the requirements for terminating an operation, including post-conflict peace-building, inevitably are more ambitious than the initial aim to avoid or halt mass atrocities?

Are there plausible responses for the inevitable criticisms of inconsistency across cases where intervention did not or cannot occur?

Is there a plan for military burden-sharing and diplomatic support from regional organizations?

The last bullet is a relatively new consideration in Washington and circumscribes future options, especially when humanitarian rather than vital interests are on the line. The scorned "leading from behind" strategy in Libya actually meant complementing U.S. military assets with those from NATO partners backed by regional diplomatic support from the Arab League, GCC and the AU. The U.S. remained essential—NATO allies still depended throughout on American precision munitions, refueling aircraft and reconnaissance. With massive cuts looming in the budget, future military action will require comparable pooling of resources; and the politics of mobilizing regional support will require multilateral cooperation. "Perhaps it's better understood as leading without wishing to be seen as taking the lead," muses the *New York Times Magazine's* Jim Traub, "a new model of multilateralism suitable to a post-hegemonic era."

Conclusion

Dilemmas remain as Libya—a country with no history of democracy and plenty of ethnic feuds and bitterness—hurtles headlong into a new era; Côte d'Ivoire is returning displaced persons, soothing memories of massacres and alleviating human suffering; and Syria continues to hemorrhage. Military force is neither a panacea nor a cause for celebration. It remains unusual for the U.S. or other countries to come to the rescue militarily although hard power remains an essential arrow in the quiver.

In the abstract, R2P clearly indicates that state sovereignty is no longer absolute. If a government violates international law and in particular if it permits

atrocities or perpetrates abuse, claims to authoritative policymaking may be reviewed and restricted by the Security Council. Expecting consistency is a fool's errand. In terms of applying the emerging norm, Syria is not Libya and Sri Lanka is not Côte d'Ivoire. Political interests vary. Military intervention is not a favored option when a quagmire looms. A foreign venture costing the lives of their military personnel is difficult to sustain. Gary Bass's history of *Freedom's Battle: The Origins of Humanitarian Intervention* concludes, "We are all atrocitarians now—but so far only in words and not yet in deeds." Libya modifies his conclusion: no longer "only" but "overwhelmingly" in words and "too rarely" in deeds. The use of armed force for protection purposes had largely disappeared from the international agenda until Libya and Côte d'Ivoire; yet deployment appears implausible and infeasible in Syria. For the moment, at least, the "why not" in Syria largely consists of the obverse—opposition from Russia and China and an extremely messy situation inside the country and surrounding region that forebodes negative outweighing positive consequences.

Actions by the United Nations in both Libya and Côte d'Ivoire, together with the agonizing attempts to avert Syria's descent into civil war, nonetheless suggest how far the R2P norm has come in framing decisions by states and inter-governmental organizations. The Security Council made precedent-setting operational references against Libya early in 2011: UNSCR 1970 had unanimous support for a substantial package of measures (arms embargo, asset freeze, travel bans and reference of the situation to the ICC); and no country voted against UNSCR 1973, which imposed the no-fly zone. In addition, the Human Rights Council referred to R2P for the first time in resolution S-15/1, which led to the General Assembly's resolution 65/60 that suspended Libyan membership, the first time any elected member state had been so sanctioned. Security Council decisions concerning Côte d'Ivoire also evoked the spirit of R2P. This was particularly apparent in the authorization embodied in resolution 1951—and re-affirmed in subsequent resolutions—to bolster UNOCI's capacity with re-deployments from the UN mission in Liberia and the provision of additional police and military capabilities. Critically, 10 council decisions have involved the R2P norm and six of those took place in 2011 and a seventh in 2012.

Carl von Clausewitz, the father of modern military strategy, is the usual point of departure for analysts who argue that diplomats should step aside when negotiations fail and let soldiers pursue politics by other means, war. Ironically, intervention justified by R2P requires that diplomats succeed in securing agreement either on preventive measures or on the deployment of military force. In the latter case, diplomats stand aside after they have succeeded and soldiers do what diplomats cannot—halt mass atrocities.

It is worth revisiting what happened to the passion and commitment of President Bill Clinton's *mea culpa* after Rwanda. Washington and London's disingenuous "humanitarian" justifications for the Iraq war were temporarily a conversation stopper for R2P. In addition, mounting the bully pulpit disappeared from job descriptions in the UN secretariat under Ban Ki-moon. The acceptable middle ground shifted away from the view that there was too little too late in terms of using military force to halt the murder of some 800,000 Rwandans. Until Libya, the United Nations leaned in the direction of the critics of the so-called new militarism—a minority in the global South that condemns R2P as a Trojan horse of Western neo-imperialism.

Today the challenge of R2P is not inadequate consensus. The red herring of imperialism is often tossed into the diplomatic pond. There is ample cultural evidence across the global South to sustain robust and justifiable humanitarian action; and support by countries in the region for outside intervention in Libya was noteworthy and perhaps a harbinger, as was fulsome rhetorical support by regional organizations for action in Côte d'Ivoire and Syria. The worry that the powerful seek an excuse to intervene

TOM/CARTOONARTS INTERNATIONAL

CartoonArts International: www.nytsyn.com/cartoons

is misplaced. As the moral philosopher Michael Walzer observes, "It is more often the case that powerful states don't do enough, or don't do anything at all, in response to desperate need than that they respond in imperialist ways."

Perhaps policymakers will recognize that there was not too much military intervention for human protection purposes but rather nothing significant between Kosovo in 1999 and Libya in 2011. Politics and military capacity ultimately determine whether, when, where and why to protect and assist affected populations. However shocking to the conscience a particular emergency and however hard or soft the applicable international law, when political will and a military capacity exist, humanitarian space will open and war victims will be assisted and protected. In Libya the moral, legal, political and military dimensions dovetailed under the responsibility to protect. Rather than speaking truth to power, R2P's value-added was speaking truth *with* power.

Along with tougher sanctions on Iran and ending the disastrous war in Iraq, American participation in Libya is one of the few signature successes of the administration's foreign policy. Speaking in Brazil after imposing the no-fly zone, Obama saw no contradiction with his premature Nobel Peace Prize—one can favor peace but still authorize force to halt the "butchering"

of civilians. The president's decision prevented massacres that would have, in his words, "stained the conscience of the world."

The results of the November elections provide a second wind for the president's earlier commitment to multilateralism. Temporarily muted by the domestic preoccupations of an electoral campaign, multilateral cooperation in the second Obama administration should make a comeback because international legitimacy is a form of power. U.S. leadership is not best exercised through the unilateral assertion of dominance in a world increasingly less supportive of such arrogance.

Hopefully, Libya was not an aberration. Although Syria currently shames international inaction and appears to dash the hopes for decisive intervention, human abattoirs are not inevitable. We are capable of uttering no more Holocausts, Cambodias and Rwandas—and occasionally mean it. "Never again" has been theorized *ad nauseam* in diplomatic gatherings and university seminars from Boston to Benghazi; but U.S. leadership makes it a plausible proposition. And if Assad leaves Syria, it will in part reflect the growing traction of the R2P norm. ∎

✔ **Opinion Ballots**
after page 32

discussion questions

1. How has the R2P doctrine evolved since its emergence in December 2001? Do you agree that it is a moral responsibility? Have specific cases reflected poorly or positively on the concept of R2P? Is there a consensus among governments about R2P and when it should be invoked? When it comes to intervention grounded in the R2P doctrine, is international cooperation essential?

2. Recent experiences in Somalia, Rwanda and Libya, among others, conjure up strong emotions among many Americans. Has the U.S. done enough in supporting R2P or has it done too much? Should the U.S. step back and allow other countries to lead international efforts? Relative to other U.S. interests, how should R2P be prioritized?

3. The author states that it is difficult to come to a conclusion over whether or not the "international action in Libya has definitively accelerated the internalization of the [R2P] norm." Do you agree with the application of R2P in Libya? What are the implications about the absence of intervention in Syria? What significance do these events have on the viability of the R2P doctrine?

4. The author states that, in Cote d'Ivoire and Libya, the reason for international action was that "military action was justifiable and feasible." Do you agree with this assertion? Did the benefits of international action outweigh the costs? In the context of these situations, how do you think the role of the U.S. was perceived in the international community, namely in the UN? Compared with countries such as France and Britain, should the U.S. have done more to advance intervention?

5. Is the international response in Syria "anemic," as the author states? Is the evidence presented compelling enough to intervene? What role, positive or negative, have the media and the general public in the aftermath of the Libyan intervention played in helping or hindering intervention in Syria?

6. China and Russia have vetoed a UN Security Council resolution calling for sanctions on Syria three times. If the Security Council is stalemated, what countries or institutions should bear the responsibility for R2P? Should regional organizations, such as the Arab League, step in?

suggested readings

International Commission on Intervention and State Sovereignty, **The Responsibility to Protect.** Ottawa, International Development Research Centre, 2001. 108 pp. Available free online at: <http://www.responsibilitytoprotect.org/ICISS%20Report.pdf>. This original report remains an essential point of departure along with the accompanying research volume by Thomas G. Weiss and Don Hubert, The Responsibility to Protect: Research, Bibliography, Background (Ottawa: International Development Research Centre, 2001).

Orford, Anne, **International Authority and the Responsibility to Protect.** New York, Cambridge University Press, 2011. 248 pp. $40.99 (paper). This book is characterized by a focus on public international law.

Hehir, Aidan, **The Responsibility to Protect: Rhetoric, Reality and the Future of Humanitarian Intervention.** New York: Palgrave Macmillan, 2012. 312 pp. $37.00 (paper). This book provides a more skeptical view of intervention, questioning the evolution of the responsibility to protect doctrine.

Bass, Gary J., Freedom's Battle: **The Origins of Humanitarian Intervention.** New York, Knopf, 2008. 528 pp. $35.00 (hardcover). This book provides a history of humanitarian advocacy, including military intervention.

UNHCR, **The State of the World's Refugees 2012: In Search of Solidarity.** New York, Oxford University Press, 2012. 340 pp. $35.00 (paper). This report contains authoritative and up-to-date analyses of current issues and data.

The Global Centre for the Responsibility to Protect also publishes a bi-monthly R2P Monitor available at http://globalr2p.org/.

Iran and the U.S.: three decades of futility
by John W. Limbert

Demonstrators perched atop of the United States Embassy wall burn an American flag, November 9, 1979, the fourth American flag to be burned since the students seized the Embassy and more than 50 hostages five days earlier. (BETTMANN/CORBIS)

The arrival of 2013 marks 34 years since Iran's Islamic revolution overthrew the ruling Pahlavi monarchy and established an "Islamic Republic," a form of government new for both Iran and the region. The same year also marks 33 years since the U.S. formally broke diplomatic relations with Iran. That rupture followed a militant student group's attack on the American Embassy in Tehran, the nation's capital, where they held over 50 of its employees hostage pending the return of the deposed Mohammad Reza Shah Pahlavi.

Those 34 years are unique in America's diplomatic history. Few estrangements have lasted so long or featured so much hostility without descending into open warfare. Both Iran and the U.S. have settled into patterns of thought and action that, while failing to end the estrangement, have become familiar and comfortable for their practitioners.

During this time, the leaders of the Islamic Republic have woven anti-Americanism (*amrika-setizi*) into the fabric of its political culture. Few public events can pass without anti-American slogans and without speakers reciting Iran's grievances, real or imagined, against what it calls "world arrogance" and "the great Satan." In this atmosphere, those

JOHN W. LIMBERT *holds the Class of 1955 Chair of Middle Eastern Studies at the U.S. Naval Academy. During a 34-year career in the United States Foreign Service, he served mostly in the Middle East and Islamic Africa and was Ambassador to the Islamic Republic of Mauritania. In 2009–10 he came out of retirement to serve as Deputy Assistant Secretary of State for Near Eastern (Iranian) Affairs. He has written numerous articles and books including* Iran at War with History *(Westview Press, 1987),* Shiraz in the Age of Hafez *(University of Washington Press, 2004), and* Negotiating with Iran *(U.S. Institute of Peace, 2009).*

Iranians who question the ruling system or who demand their rights as citizens face accusations of being "American mercenaries." The regime blames its many economic, political and diplomatic failures on the U.S. and on a coordinated cultural assault (*tajavoz-e-farhangi*) from a powerful but decadent West. Every year on November 4, crowds rally to commemorate the capture of the American Embassy in 1979, pretending that such an act was a positive achievement rather than an ugly violation of every Iranian's national and religious traditions. In December 2011, a group, with backing from within the system, attempted to replicate that event by attacking the British Embassy in Tehran.

The American side has reciprocated this suspicion and hostility. American politicians describe Iran variously as a "threat," a "regional hegemon," and, in President George W. Bush's memorable 2002 phrase, a member of an "axis of evil." American political figures speak of "regime change" and of how the Islamic Republic needs to "change its behavior." Congress piles on sanction after sanction with little apparent consideration of their effects on ordinary Iranians (whom the U.S. says it is supporting) or even the ultimate goal of these measures beyond expressing (in President Obama's phrase), "the satisfying purity of indignation." American officials almost gloat over cyberwar measures against Iran's nuclear program and computer networks. And agencies of the U.S. government seemed to look the other way as an officially designated Iranian terrorist group, the Mujahedeen Khalq or People's Mujahedeen (MEK/MKO), operated openly in American territory.

The iron rules

Where are American-Iranian relations today? They are about where they have been for the past three decades. The two sides continue to glare at each other from across an abyss. They trade insults, threats and empty slogans. Sometimes the exchanges go beyond words and escalate to overflights, terrorist plots and now cyberattacks. The irony is that on both sides there is recognition that this 30-year pattern is not only dysfunctional but also dangerous. When tentative steps toward change encounter difficulties—as they inevitably do—each side reverts to the sterile but familiar practices of the past. Over three decades both sides have become expert in bashing the other while unable to find a path to something more productive. They end up condemned to doing what they know best.

Decades of estrangement have taken their toll. After so much hostility, floundering and missteps, officials in both Tehran and Washington find themselves in the unwavering grip of five self-destructive rules that, like the biblical "Laws of the Medes and the Persians that alter not," are set in stone. These rules, which have come to control both sides, are:

■ Never walk through an open door. Instead, bang your head against a wall.

■ Never say yes to anything the other side proposes. Doing so will make you look weak.

■ The other side is infinitely hostile, devious, domineering and irrational. It is the embodiment of all that is evil.

■ Therefore, anything the other side proposes must contain some kind of trick. Its only purpose in life is to cheat you.

■ Whenever you seem to be making progress, someone or some diabolical coincidence will mess it up.

Much of this dangerous impasse results from the fact that the Americans and the Iranians are unable to talk to each other about matters that concern both. More than three years of the Obama administration's effort to alter this relationship brought only one high-level meeting between American and Iranian officials (the 2009 meeting between State Department official William J. Burns and Saeed Jalili, Iran's

LUCIDITY INFORMATION DESIGN, LLC

chief nuclear negotiator, in Geneva, Switzerland). The issue is not friendship; it is the mutual interests of two sovereign states communicating matters of importance without necessarily being friends. The Iranian side has convinced itself that talking to the Americans would somehow undermine the foundations of the Islamic Republic. The American side has convinced itself that talking to the Iranians outside of the narrowest format would be seen as a sign of weakness.

The result is that, failing direct communication, each side has created a distorted and demonized picture of the other. Contributing to the misreadings are the self-interested images that third parties are promoting in order to foster fear and dislike and prevent any change in a *status quo* that serves their interests. The result has been clear. Failing direct communication, each side has created an image of the other as simultaneously superhuman and subhuman: the former easy to fear, the latter easy to despise.

The ghosts of history

Matters were not always this way. American-Iranian hostility is recent and, until 1979, the relationship was mostly positive. Contacts originated in the second half of the 19th century when American missionaries in Iran (then called Persia) worked on health, education and proselytizing. They encountered an Iran that had become a de facto colony of imperial Britain and Russia. In the 18th and 19th centuries, because of military defeats and economic decline, Iran had lost territory, sovereignty and control of its resources. Cash-strapped Qajar dynasty (1785–1925) rulers, needing money for their courts and their European trips, took out loans and sold off resources ("concessions") to foreigners at fire-sale prices. Treaties ("capitulations") granted foreign private citizens and even Iranians who could somehow obtain foreign "protection," immunity from local law.

In the early 20th century Britain and Russia formally divided Persia into spheres of influence. Russia controlled Iran's only effective military force (the Persian Cossack Brigade) and Britain, following the discovery of oil in Iran's southwest, controlled its primary source of wealth. Iran's social and economic conditions put it far behind Europe, the U.S. and even the Ottoman Empire. The historian Ervand Abrahamian estimates Iran's literacy rate in 1900–06 at 5 percent. In the same period, life expectancy was 30 years and infant mortality 500 per 1,000 births. The country had 2,000 students in state schools, no universities and 12 kilometers of railroad.

In this setting, the U.S. had two factors in its favor. Most important, the U.S. was NOT Britain or Russia and did not have those countries' imperial history in Iran. Furthermore, the U.S., to the extent it was involved in Iran, appeared to sympathize with those Iranians who, from the late 19th century, had begun a struggle to regain control over their own country, limit the arbitrary power of the rulers and acquire a voice in how they were governed. In 1909, Howard Baskerville, a young American teacher at a missionary school in Tabriz, lost his life fighting alongside the constitutionalists against pro-monarchy forces and their Russian allies. In 1910–11, Morgan Shuster, an American Treasury Department official, led a team that helped Iran's new and fragile constitutional government gain control of national finances. In late 1911, the Russians forced out Shuster and his team when they attempted to collect taxes from an Iranian citizen under Russian protection.

At the same time, American missionaries established hospitals and made important contributions to Iranian education. The American Presbyterian missionary Samuel Jordan (1871–1952) established the boys' high school in Tehran that came to be known (after 1928) as Alborz College. That college—which operated as a selective public secondary school after 1943—became the training ground for Iran's intellectual elite. Many of its graduates became Iran's leaders in mathematics, engineering and the sciences. ∎

The U.S. enters Iran's political life

IRANIAN-AMERICAN relations remained limited until the World War II. Reza Shah Pahlavi (who ruled from 1925 to 1941) established nationalist policies that restricted foreign influence. The Soviet Union had renounced czarist privileges and loans and Reza Shah remained very suspicious of Communist influence. British influence, despite a renegotiation of the original 1901 concession, remained strong in the all-important oil industry.

World War II and its aftermath made America an important new factor in the Iranian political arena. The U.S. became a leading actor in a new form of the "great game," now called the cold war (1945–91). In the original 19th-century version, Britain and Czarist Russia competed for influence in Central Asia, Afghanistan and Iran. In the updated version the Soviet Union replaced imperial Russia and the U.S. took over the role formerly played by Britain. Iran, which had been just one of the pieces of this game, now became the major prize, and Iranian oil, which was not a factor in the 19th century—Baku was the only oil-producing area in the region—now became part of the stakes. Communism and anticommunism added an ideological component to the game as well.

The cold war itself began in Iran after World War II. It was no accident that three of the first five resolutions of the United Nations Security Council (numbers 2, 3 and 5, issued in 1946) concerned Iran and its difficulties with the Soviet Union. Iran was again at the center of the world stage, and the U.S.—long a minor player in Iranian affairs—was playing a new and leading role.

During their wartime occupation, the Soviets, stymied in their search for an oil concession to balance the powerful British presence in southwest Iran, encouraged separatist movements in Iranian Kurdestan and Azerbaijan. In 1945, when the Iranian central government attempted to reassert its authority in those regions, Soviet troops blocked Iranian forces from moving beyond Qazvin, only 75 miles northwest of Tehran. By the end of year, the situation for Iran was bleak. Separatists, known as the Democratic Party of Azerbaijan (DPA) were in control of the province and their Soviet backers were making no move to leave Iran as stipulated in the original tripartite treaty. The intentions of the Americans and British were unclear, but neither was prepared to keep forces in the country as a counterweight to the Soviet presence in the north.

According to the standard Iranian version of events, the Soviets withdrew from Iran in response to an ultimatum from President Harry S. Truman. Although the Americans did offer Iran diplomatic support at the Allies' foreign ministers Moscow conference in December 1945 and at the United Nations in early 1946, there is no evidence of any American ultimatum. The U.S. did not want to see the Soviets remain in Iran indefinitely or establish a puppet state in the northwest; but President Truman was not prepared to go beyond the diplomatic steps noted.

After the war, the U.S. would have preferred to resume its traditional role as a minor player in Iranian affairs. However, the growing competition with the Soviet Union drew Washington into Iranian domestic politics in a new way. In 1947, for example, the U.S. decided to back the young Shah Mohammad Reza Pahlavi in a power struggle with his powerful Prime Minister Ahmad Qavam. Although Qavam had successfully maneuvered through the interlocking crises of 1945–47, neither the British nor the Americans trusted him.

The former believed he had his eye on ending the lucrative British oil concession and the latter considered him and his political allies too friendly to the Soviet Union. In December 1947 Qavam resigned and left the country.

The political scientist Richard Cottam summarizes American entry into Iran's domestic affairs as follows:

American diplomacy in the war years and immediately after was already reflecting U.S. ambivalence with regard to involvement in Iran's internal affairs. [Financial adviser] Arther Millspaugh was one American without ambivalence. Iranians needed, he made clear, a long period of tutelage….But U.S. ambassadors Murray and Allen consistently rejected explicit appeals from the shah and others to play the interventionist role this formula called for. Yet day by day the matters taken up by the ambassadors with Iranian officials moved more deeply into matters of domestic policy concerns.

From friend to puppet master

As the cold war continued, American policy in Iran came to focus on one overriding goal: keeping the Communists out. That goal meant excluding them from Iranian territory, from the Iranian government and from Iranian oil.

That goal became the "prime directive" of America's Iran policy and shaped Washington's reaction to the tumultuous events of 1951–53 during the crisis surrounding the nationalization of the Anglo-Iranian Oil Company (AIOC) and the premiership of the National Front leader Mohammad Mosaddegh. For Mosaddegh and his allies the issue was simple: putting their country's single most important resource under Iranian control. On the British side, the oil company insisted on upholding the letter of earlier, one-sided agreements and fought doggedly against any arrangement that would threaten its monopoly control. Although some in the British government sympathized with Iranian nationalists, officials came to personalize their disagreement and see Mosaddegh himself as the problem.

In their view he was "the wrong kind of Persian"—hopelessly xenophobic, stubborn and irrational.

In the summer of 1951, President Truman, faced with a dispute between two friends that threatened to become an open conflict, attempted mediation. Both sides, however, had dug themselves into positions where agreement was impossible. The Iranians became captive to their own anti-British rhetoric and seemed to prefer no solution to compromise. The British, for their part, identified Mosaddegh himself as the source of the dispute and decided that he had to go and be replaced with someone more "reasonable."

Although there was considerable American sympathy for the Iranian position, Mosaddegh and the National Front in the end fell victim to cold-war calculations and American domestic politics. Mosaddegh never seemed to appreciate the realities of the American political scene, while the British skillfully played on the rampant fears of communism that were poisoning American politics. Washington was bogged down in an unpopular war in Korea; China and Eastern Europe had fallen under Communist control; and Senator Joseph R. McCarthy (R–Wis.), chanting slogans about "treason" against the Democrats, was on the rampage. The Republicans, with McCarthy's help, had routed Democrats in the 1950 congressional elections.

Mosaddegh saw little of this American reality. Instead he considered the Americans straightforward people without deeper motives who would eventually see the justice of the Iranian case. He failed to recognize the forces that drove Truman and later President Dwight D. Eisenhower to throw Iran and the National Front to the wolves. In November 1952 a National Security Council study concluded that there was a real danger of a Communist takeover in Iran and that Mosaddegh and his National Front, by their incompetence, were incapable of stopping it. The study noted,

Present trends in Iran are unfavorable to the maintenance of control by a non-Communist regime for an

extended period of time. In wrestling the political initiative from the shah, the landlords and other traditional holders of power, the National Front politicians now in power have at least temporarily eliminated every alternative to their own rule except the Communist Tudeh Party. However, the ability of the National Front to maintain control of the situation indefinitely is uncertain. The political upheaval which brought the nationalists to power has heightened popular desire for promised economic and social betterment and has increased social unrest....

Any U.S. policy regarding Iran must accordingly take into account the danger that the Communists might be enabled to gain the ascendency....It is clear that the United Kingdom no longer possesses the capability unilaterally to assure stability in the area. If present trends continue unchecked, Iran could be effectively lost to the free world in advance of an actual Communist takeover of the Iranian government. Failure to arrest present trends in Iran involves a serious risk to the national security of the U.S.

Once the Eisenhower administration came to office in January 1953 it was an easy move for the militantly anticommunist Dulles brothers (John Foster and Allen) to shift from the concern of their Democratic predecessors to ordering the Central Intelligence Agency (CIA) to join the British in a covert plan to remove Mosaddegh. In March President Eisenhower approved the plan, and CIA and British agents in Tehran began plotting the operation (code-named "Ajax"). That operation climaxed in August 1953 with a coup that replaced Mosaddegh with General Fazlollah Zahedi and began 25 years of royal control and American influence that would end only with the Islamic Revolution of 1979.

It is difficult to overestimate the effects of the 1953 events on the Iranians' view of themselves and their relations with the outside world. Most Iranians, of whatever political opinion, see the events as treachery by a country they

Iranian Premier Mohammed Mossadegh rides on the shoulders of cheering crowds in Tehran's Majlis Square on Sept. 27, 1951, outside the parliament building, after reiterating his oil nationalization views to his public supporters. (AP)

imagined was a friend or at least free of the old colonial arrogance. It was nothing new for Iranians to see themselves as victims of injustice and powerful, malevolent outside forces. What they did not expect, however, was that the Americans, in the eight years from 1945 to 1953, would go from major backer of Iranian independence to coup maker and betrayer of Iranian aspirations for dignity and self-respect.

The tragedy of these events still casts a shadow over Iranian-American relations. The British, the Americans and the Iranians all saw the oil nationalization controversy very differently and failed to comprehend the views of the other side. To the British, the Iranians, particularly Mosaddegh ("Mad Mossy" as the editorialists called him), were exasperating, the antithesis of everything the British admired in themselves: they ignored the sanctity of contracts and were ungrateful, emotional and irrational. They were, in short, a lesser species of human being. In the words of one British scholar of Iran, "Really, it seemed hardly fair that dignified and correct Western statesmanship should be defeated by the antics of incomprehensible Orientals."

When forced to choose between the Iranians and the British, the Americans

seemed more comfortable with the latter. Both sides in the oil dispute had dug themselves into inflexible positions and the Americans saw little room for agreement. Fear of advancing world communism and toxic domestic politics worsened the situation and made Washington sacrifice Iranian nationalism on the altar of the new great game and cold-war geopolitics. Dean Acheson and John Foster Dulles (both secretaries of state) viewed the world through anticommunist lenses and could not appreciate what lay behind apparent Iranian "irrationality." Although many American observers criticized British inflexibility on the oil issue, there was little understanding of how the Iranians saw the dispute, which was not only in terms of an oil agreement, but about regaining their national self-respect lost for almost two centuries.

A bad marriage

The next 25 years were years of little wisdom for both Tehran and Washington. After the 1953 coup the shah and U.S. were stuck with each other for better or worse. The shah, in the view of many of his subjects, could do nothing right. His rule was tainted by the fact that he owed his throne to foreign intervention. Nothing he could do would shake that perception and all his actions, good or bad, were viewed ultimately as done on instructions from Washington. His actions, as interpreted by many Iranians, had one priority: to stay in power by pleasing his foreign masters. As for the shah, he remained convinced that his grip on power depended on the goodwill of outsiders, who had helped his father gain power in 1921, removed his father in 1941, put him on the throne the same year, backed him against Qavam in 1947 and toppled Mosaddegh in 1953.

The Americans were equally stuck, although they were sometimes uneasy with their Iranian friend. It was hard to hide the corruption, brutality and authoritarianism of the Pahlavi court. Yet American officials of both parties repeatedly fêted the shah in Washington and represented him as the "linchpin" of American anticommunist policy in the region. Not wanting to criticize a rare friend in the Middle East, American presidents rarely mentioned human rights, democracy and honest government.

This close relationship, however, led both sides to make dubious assumptions and act thoughtlessly. Throughout the 1960's and 1970's, the shah's policies, especially those fueled by high oil prices after 1973, seemed to lurch about

aimlessly. In the 1970s he decided Iran should have "agro-industry"; in 1975 he decreed a one-party system; in 1977–78 he changed the clock and the Iranian-Islamic calendar. The Americans did little better and seemed blind to the effects of their actions. In 1963–64 they compelled the shah to accept changes to the existing "Status of Forces Agreement" (SOFA) that regulated the legal conditions of American military personnel stationed in Iran. The new agreement extended immunities to the family members of American technical advisers and provoked a storm of protest about a new regime of hated "capitulations." The controversy gave Ayatollah Khomeini, until then a cleric who focused his opposition on social and religious issues, his start in nationalist politics. His outspoken opposition to the SOFA—opposition that led to his exile in November 1964—earned him great respect among Iranian intellectuals who came to overlook his extremist views on the role of religion in politics.

Although American officials might publicly deny the client status of the shah, it was sometimes difficult for them to resist treating him like one. It was also easy for Americans to ignore Iranian public opinion for some other interest, large or small. In the 1970's,

for example, tens of thousands of Americans worked in Iran for defense contractors such as Bell Helicopter and created resentment by acts that offended local sensibilities in an Islamic society. On a larger scale, President Richard M. Nixon's 1973 appointment of CIA chief Richard Helms to be ambassador to Tehran sent a clear message to Iranians: the U.S. is showing you who is in charge of your country and it will not even make a pretense of respecting your sovereignty. Washington seemed to glory in its cluelessness and mistook Iranians' sullen silence as acceptance. When all the grievances surfaced in 1978–79, American officials were caught completely by surprise and had no idea of the cumulative resentments built up by previous thoughtless decisions.

The party ends

The bill for all of this ignorance and self-indulgence came due in 1978–79. As long as the shah welcomed American business, supported anticommunist policies and purchased expensive American weapons systems, Washington was content to ignore other unpleasant realities. In late 1977 and early 1978, Iran, buttressed by high oil prices, appeared strong and stable. It had no foreign enemies and had even settled long-running disputes with Baghdad (at the expense of Iraq's Kurdish population) and Bahrain. There were economic difficulties and political problems, but the shah had always shown himself able to weather such storms. President and Mrs. Jimmy Carter saw Iran and the shah as attractive enough to spend New Year's eve of 1977–78 as guests of the shah in Tehran, where the President, in his toast, made his famous statement about Iran's being "an island of stability in one of the more troubled areas of the world."

President Carter left Tehran in January 1978. Just over one year later Iran was in revolutionary chaos, the exiled Khomeini had returned in triumph, the shah was gone, and his government, army and security forces finally collapsed on February 11, 1979. The next day, Washington woke up with a huge collective hangover. The party was

President and Mrs. Carter escort the Shah and Shahbanou of Iran to a state dinner in the White House, 1977. (CORBIS)

over and now President Carter and his administration—who had been caught completely off guard by the revolution—had to figure out how do deal with the new Iranian reality.

As Carter's advisers flailed around looking for a policy that made sense, two important lines of thought emerged. One said that the Iranian revolution had not changed the underlying geopolitics of U.S. strategy and that Washington could (and should) adjust to the changes in Tehran. In this view, the prime directive of anticommunism still applied and the cold war competition with the Soviets still dominated Washington's thinking about Iran. There might be new rulers in Tehran, but the Soviet Union was still the enemy, the great game continued and Iran remained one of its top prizes.

In those circumstances, it was important to salvage something from the turmoil in Iran. Bilateral relations could not be what they once were, but there were still important American interests at stake, including major weapons sales. It was vital, therefore, that the Americans show the Iranians that Washington had "accepted" the revolution.

With all of the uncertainty, there were promising signs that conditions might settle down in the coming months. The new interim prime minister, his cabinet and many officials were basically religious intellectuals, many with a history of National Front political activity. Few were extreme religious or leftist ideologues. In private conversations, many showed appreciation for Iran's broader national interests and continuing some kind of relationship with the U.S. that protected those interests.

A second, more pessimistic view saw the Iranian revolution as an unmitigated disaster for Washington. An important ally had fallen, the U.S. appeared helpless and indecisive and there was nothing to be salvaged from this catastrophe. "Coming to terms" with Iran's revolution was an exercise in futility. The only sensible course of action was unmitigated hostility to the new rulers in Tehran. This view did not minimize the Soviet threat, but believed that the Soviets would take full advantage of the

A boy in camouflage fatigues points a toy pistol at an effigy of U.S. President Carter, during a demonstration outside of the U.S. Embassy in Tehran, Iran, November 18, 1979. The effigy was topped with empty cartons of American-made cigarettes boycotted by Iranians after the U.S. Embassy was stormed and hostages taken on November 3, 1979. (AFP/GETTY IMAGES)

chaos and prevailing anti-Americanism in Tehran.

As time passed, conditions on the ground seemed to support the more pessimistic view. The atmosphere in Tehran became increasingly hostile to those seeking a return to normality and the country was lurching toward mob rule. The shouts of extremists on left and right were drowning out the voices of those—including key members of the provisional government—who were calling for reestablishing an organized society, protecting economic infrastructure and preserving orderly relations with the outside world. Power was falling into the hands of a shadowy collection of "revolutionary" institutions that ignored the authority of the provisional government. By the summer and fall of 1979, street gangs, neighborhood vigilantes, revolutionary courts, revolutionary guards and Friday prayer leaders were taking control of events in Iran. Revolutionary courts dispensed rapid and dubious justice. Local vigilantes and revolutionary guards shut down newspapers and arrested whom they pleased. The media became increasingly strident and almost hysterical. Voices on both the left and right called for more trials, more executions and a radical remaking of Iranian society. At the same time, as-

sassinations and ongoing clashes in the provinces and on university campuses, led to louder denunciation of "American mercenaries."

The collapse

By the fall of 1979, U.S.-Iranian relations were on the edge of a cliff and required only a small push for a total collapse. On October 20, 1979, the U.S. supplied that push when President Carter gave in to his advisers and agreed to admit the deposed shah to the U.S. for emergency treatment of his cancer. Less than two weeks later, on November 4, a mob calling itself "Moslem Student Followers of the Imam's Line" overran the American Embassy, captured the American staff members and announced it was holding them hostage for the return of the shah.

Prime Minister Mehdi Bazargan's provisional government was unable to act. Ayatollah Khomeini, sensing the prevailing hysteria, decided to ride the political wave and endorsed the occupation as a "second revolution greater than the first." He and his followers then used the event to consolidate their power and drive their rivals, including secular nationalists and religious intellectuals, into the political wilderness. Bazargan and his cabinet found themselves helpless before a tide of mob rule

Iranian protestors hold a up a poster of Ayatollah Khomeini during a demonstration against the Shah in Tehran, January, 1979. (AFP/GETTY IMAGES)

and resigned. Iran was effectively without a government and what had begun as a 1970's-style student sit-in became a huge international crisis. Washington broke diplomatic relations with Tehran in April 1980 and the two sides began their bitter estrangement that has lasted over three decades.

The hostage crisis dragged on for 14 months, complicated by Iran's refusal to speak directly to the U.S., by the bloody Iran-Iraq war (1980–88) and by Iran's vicious internal strife that paralyzed any effort at consistent diplomacy. A settlement brokered by Algerian mediators did not lead to a resumption of American-Iranian contact, even on issues of common interest. Iranians remained consumed by their domestic struggles and purges, particularly the bloody battles with the MEK/MKO and other leftist groups. On the American side, the events—compounded by catastrophes in Lebanon—left such a bitter taste that successive administrations preferred to ignore Iran. As the historian Ali Ansari put it, "Any proponents [of seeking areas of agreement with Iran]—in some cases diplomats who had been held hostage in 1979—were treated like the thesis they espoused, as delusional."

Years of futility

Try as they might, American administrations could not ignore the Islamic Republic, which had an unpleasant habit of intruding on American consciousness. The ghosts of 1953, 1979 and other events remained unexorcised. Unable to ignore Iran, Washington tried everything else: dealing with it, changing it, containing it and talking with it. Nothing worked and the two sides remained locked in bitter and unproductive exchanges of insults, threats and pointless slogans. Ironically, each frustrated effort to change the relationship made the hostility even worse. Each failure confirmed one side's suspicion and demonization of the other and led to the explanation, "Well, we tried, but THEY are just too irrational/arrogant/unreasonable/suspicious/hostile."

Iran has become a nightmare for suc-

cessive American presidents, who have been forced to deal with its unpleasant reality. To paraphrase Russia's Leon Trotsky ("You may have no business with war; but war has business with you"), American presidents may have hoped to have no business with Iran. But Iran has had business with them. Here is the sad record of American Administrations after 1979:

■ Jimmy Carter lost his presidency in 1980, in large part because of the Tehran embassy hostage crisis.

■ Ronald Reagan came within an eyelash of losing his office because of the Iran-contra scandal of 1986, in which dubious intermediaries convinced a White House obsessed with the Soviet threat that it should support (nonexistent) anticommunist groups in Tehran with arms supplies.

■ George H.W. Bush had to eat his inaugural address words "goodwill begets goodwill" after the Iranians helped end the captivity of American hostages in Lebanon. After Iranian President Hashemi Rafsanjani helped arrange their freedom in 1991, he was informed that there was no American goodwill to be had.

■ Bill Clinton's efforts at "dual containment" of Iran and Iraq went nowhere and his attempted outreach to Iranian President Mohammad Khatami (1997–2005) came to nothing. In response to Khatami's new tone of civil discourse begun in 1998, the Clinton administration proposed negotiations without preconditions to develop a road map to better relations. The offer was apparently a bridge too far for the Iranian side, which rejected the proposal.

■ Under President George W. Bush, in 2001–02 Iranian and American diplomats cooperated effectively to create a new political structure for Afghanistan after the fall of the Taliban. Rather than bring further progress, however, this move was followed, in January 2002, by his State of the Union address which put Iran, Iraq and North Korea into the "axis of evil."

■ In May 2003 the Iranians, through the Swiss Embassy in Tehran, submitted a proposal for talks on a wide range of issues of concern to both sides. The Bush Administration, confident from its apparently easy military victory in Iraq, ignored the proposal and never responded. Eventually the Iranians themselves denied they had made such an offer.

■ Barack Obama began his Administration in 2009 with serious efforts at changing the bilateral relationship, but bad luck, bad timing, impatience and mutual suspicions have frustrated his efforts. ■

Iran and Obama: poetry, greetings and mutual respect

DURING HIS 2008 presidential campaign, Barack Obama advocated a new approach to Iran, saying that sometimes American interests required dealing with adversaries. In the case of Iran, his stand earned him harsh criticism from both his Democratic primary rival Hillary Clinton and the Republican candidate John McCain. Obama made it clear, however, that he was determined to change what was, for him, a 30-year-old policy that had produced nothing positive. In his inaugural address, the president said, "To the Muslim world, we seek a new way forward based on mutual respect." Six days later he told an interviewer from Dubai-based *Al-Arabiyya* television that problems in the Middle East originated in "negative preconceptions." Although he did not mention Iran explicitly his meaning was clear: as long as Iranians and Americans assume the worst about each other, there will be no chance to end their long and costly estrangement.

President Obama continued his outreach efforts. He made his earlier, general points explicitly to Iran in his March 2009 Nowruz (Iranian New Year) greetings. In that message he signaled a major rhetorical change when he spoke directly to the government of the "Islamic Republic of Iran" (using the official name) as well as to its people. He called for "engagement that is honest and grounded in mutual respect." He quoted the 13th century Persian poet Sa'adi,

The children of Adam are limbs of one body,
Which God created from one essence.

In his June 4, 2009, Cairo speech, Obama called for a "new beginning" between the U.S. and the Muslim world, based upon mutual interest and mutual respect." He amplified the message for Iran. Acknowledging the difficulties of overcoming decades of mistrust, he said that Washington was willing to deal with Iran "without preconditions and on the basis of mutual respect."

With Iran, Obama was hitting all the right notes. He did not threaten or bluster. In a reasonable world, his approach would have brought results. He was addressing all that the Iranians said they wanted to begin a dialogue, including the elusive concept of "respect." His talk of mutual respect addressed a long-held Iranian view that their country was the "Rodney Dangerfield of the Middle East" and did not receive the respect owed its economic, political, cultural and geostrategic importance. His using the official name "Islamic Republic of Iran" and his addressing its leaders was a clear signal that the U.S. was no longer saying that the only good Islamic Republic was a toppled one. Nor was the new American government still saying to Iran, "We love your people; we detest your government." The quotation from Sa'adi was a clear acknowledgement that the President knew he was dealing with the heirs of a great civilization and culture distinct from (and in their view greater than) others in the region.

The new face of American policy under Obama caught the Iranians off guard. They did not know how to react. His message threatened to discredit Tehran's usual anti-American bombast and the leaders of the Islamic Republic found themselves facing an American

President Obama delivers his much-anticipated message to the Muslim world from the auditorium in the Cairo University campus during a one-day visit to Egypt on June 4, 2009. Obama said that he wants "a new beginning" with the world's 1.5 billion Muslims, and called for an end to a cycle of "suspicion and discord." (MANDEL NGAN/ AFP/GETTY IMAGES)

president who did not fall into the easy category of enemy. Obama's efforts, however quickly ran afoul of both accumulated mistrust and domestic turmoil in Iran. Only a few days after his June 2009 Cairo speech, Iran held presidential elections. When the authorities announced that incumbent president Mahmoud Ahmadinejad had received over 60 percent of votes in the first round, there was a storm of protest from Iranians claiming the election was stolen and shouting, "Where is my vote?" Millions of Iranians demonstrated and the authorities, after initial hesitation, unleashed a wave of repression using its goon squads, the paramilitary *basij* and revolutionary guards, to silence opposition. The regime also lashed out against the Iranian intelligentsia, arresting journalists, writers, filmmakers, bloggers, human rights lawyers and activists. It grouped all opposition and criticism into the category of "sedition" (*fetneh*) and claimed opponents and critics were participating in a "soft overthrow" campaign fomented by the Western "three letter" groups: CIA, MI-5 (British security service), BBC (British Broadcasting Corporation), VOA (Voice of

> "We've done as much diplomatically as we can realistically do. Now the question is: Is there a bargain that allows Iran to save enough face, and the West can be satisfied with?"
> —Anne-Marie Slaughter, Former Director of Policy Planning, U.S. Department of State

www.GreatDecisions.org/DVD

America) and NGOs (nongovernmental organizations).

Despite frustrations and the increasing repression in Iran, Obama did not give up. He noted in his Nobel Prize acceptance speech in December 2009 (without naming Iran) that relations with repressive regimes were important even if such engagement "lacks the satisfying purity of indignation." His efforts did not bring results, however, but instead ran into a wall of suspicion on the Iranian side and old habits on the American side. As the scholar Trita Parsi writes,

Despite extensive outreach, clear strategic benefits and an unprecedented opportunity for engagement, Obama found himself stuck in the same confrontational relationship with Iran as that of other American Presidents before him….[Under] Obama's watch, the cycle of escalation and counterescalation continues with no sign of solution in the offing.

Despite a promising start, in less than a year both sides had fallen into the dysfunctional patterns of the past. When they encountered difficulties, they reverted to what they knew best— bashing the other side.

Complications: Israel, the nuclear issue and sanctions

The two sides, while recognizing common interests in areas such as antinarcotics, antipollution, Afghanistan and Iraq, have been unable to use these common interests to change the futile practices of three decades. In addition to accumulated mistrust and hostility, Iran's extreme anti-Israeli rhetoric mixed with Holocaust denial, has fed fears in Europe, Israel and the U.S. that the Islamic Republic is a reincarnation of Nazi Germany and that its very existence threatens the survival of Israel. This anxiety has become especially strong since Ahmadinejad became president of Iran in 2005 and began repeating earlier statements from Khomeini about how Israel should be erased from the pages of time.

Why has Iran's president raised temperatures with such apparently self-de-

structive language? With his rhetoric Ahmadinejad may be appealing for support to a populist, anti-Semitic base within Iran. He may also be seeking support in Arab countries by taking an anti-Israeli stand more defiant than those of Arab governments. Whatever his motives, the effects have been as follows:

■ Some Israeli politicians are using these statements to spread fear, gain votes and claim that Iran presents an existential threat and must be stopped by any means possible, including military action.

■ Other voices in Iran—including Ahmadinejad's rivals in the 2009 presidential elections—have criticized his rhetoric as provocative and likely to lead Iran into a destructive conflict with powerful enemies.

■ Voices in the West claim that Iran is simply too fanatic and irrational to deal with and that it will be impossible to make any agreement with people who say "such things." According to these voices, President Obama's efforts at engagement with such a government and its leaders are doomed to failure. The only reasonable course of action is to destroy the Islamic Republic as soon as possible.

■ Ahmadinejad and the Islamic Republic have become the perfect enemy for Israel and its friends in the U.S. In an application of rule #5 (see above, p. 72) the Iranian president can be relied on to say something outrageous that will undermine efforts to improve relations and will in turn justify the most inflexible and aggressive stand against Iran.

Given Israel's history and the manner of its founding, such statements have created anxiety that Israel is facing a threat to its very existence from a group of irrational and fanatical leaders in Tehran determined to develop nuclear weapons. In such a setting, it has become almost impossible for the U.S.—as a strong supporter of Israel—to consider its relations with Iran as a strictly bilateral issue. Instead, Israeli-Iranian hostility has come to influence American policy and decisionmaking toward both countries. That same hostility has also influenced American domestic politics, as the President's rivals accuse him of being "soft on Iran" and of following policies that endanger America's Israeli allies in the Middle East.

It is difficult to understand what is real and what is not in this tangle of arguments. Is, for example, a potential Iranian nuclear weapon actually more dangerous than an existing nuclear arsenal in Pakistan? Is a nuclear-armed Pakistan—with a record of its military and intelligence services supporting dangerous groups and individuals—less threatening than an Iran which may or may not be building such weapons? Israeli Prime Minister Benjamin Netanyahu insists that the U.S. should declare a "red line" and announce that Iran **cannot have the capacity** to build a nuclear weapon. That very capacity, he insists, constitutes a threat to Israel's survival. President Obama, for his part, rejects talk of "red lines" but has repeatedly stated that it is "unacceptable" for Iran **to possess** a nuclear weapon.

A nuclear nondialogue

Adding to the climate of suspicion is the complex issue of Iran's nuclear program. Although the Iranians have long claimed that the program is entirely peaceful, the prevailing suspicion has left many convinced that the "duplicitous" Iranians must be hiding something. For much of the outside world, the concerns about Iran's program are technical and legal: How many centrifuges? How much low-enriched uranium (LEU)? Is Iran bound by Article 3.1 and the Additional Protocol of the 1968 Nuclear Non-Proliferation Treaty (NPT)? For Iran, however, the issues are not technical or legal but rather political and psychological—matters of national pride, respect and sovereignty. Many Iranians have claimed that they are asking for nothing more than what other countries such as Switzerland and Japan are allowed. They see themselves being treated, as they were in 1953, as an inferior species of human being.

In this atmosphere the issue has become a case study in how two sides talk past each other and engage in "asymmetric negotiations." One side speaks of "rights" while the other speaks of "ob-

Iranian President Mahmoud Ahmadinejad waves a sign reading "Down With Israel" during a demonstration marking the 32nd anniversary of the Islamic revolution in Freedom Square, Iran, February 11, 2011. (ATTA KENARE/AFP/GETTY IMAGES)

ligations." As a result, both sides leave negotiating sessions frustrated, claiming, "We are being reasonable, but the other side is just not listening." The sad reality is that for Iran the nuclear issue has become a matter of national pride and self-respect. As such it will be very difficult for any Iranian official to make the sort of agreement requested by the P5+1 (the permanent members of the UN Security Council plus Germany), to say nothing of the Israelis, and survive in the Iranian political arena. Discussing the failed Geneva agreements of October 2009, Ahmadinejad told an Iranian audience that those agreements were a good deal for Iran, but that Iran

had to reject them because the other side talked about them as though Iran had surrendered. Such a formula Iran could never accept.

Two tracks or one?

Beginning in 2010, faced with the failure of the Geneva nuclear deal and with growing frustration, the Obama administration announced it was following a "two-track" policy with Iran. While continuing to seek engagement, it would apply pressure in the form of escalating economic sanctions. In June the UN Security Council approved a sanctions resolution (UN Security Council resolution 1929); the 27-member European Union (EU) and other American allies joined in oil industry and financial sanctions that went beyond what the United Nations had approved; and Congress imposed its own set of unilateral sanctions and threatened measures against foreign countries and companies that continued to make deals with Iran.

In reality Obama's two-track policy was nothing of the sort. There was only one track. The diplomacy of sanctions, whether at the United Nations, in Washington, or in foreign capitals, took all the air out of the room and there was no time, energy, or interest in pursuing any alternative. Since 1979, successive administrations had always used sanctions with Iran. The process may have been difficult, but it was familiar. Completely unfamiliar, however, was any path to changing the iron rules and ending 30 years of futility. As Parsi explains,

…The heavy investment in the sanctions process helped to turn the matter into one of prestige. Not imposing sanctions would have been hailed as a victory by Iran and condemned by Israel and its allies in the U.S. as a sign of Obama's weakness and indecisiveness. And the more Iran pushed against the sanctions, the harder the U.S. pushed back and the more important the imposition of sanctions became.

Have the sanctions worked? It depends on who is asked. American officials have described the sanctions as "biting, crippling and punishing." The question is: who is being crippled, bitten and punished? And when officials say that sanctions against Iran are "working" what do they mean? Working for what goal? Does the U.S. want—as it says it does—sanctions to persuade the Iranians to enter a dialogue based on mutual interest and mutual respect? Or has the U.S. given up on mutual respect, intending the sanctions to batter the Iranian economy so hard that Tehran gives in to Washington's demands? Or does the U.S. want the sanctions to be another means toward regime change and to create so much hardship in Iran that the Islamic Republic collapses?

The result is an illustration of the old saying, "If you don't know where you're going, any road will get you there." Because of this uncertainty about goals, different groups with different agendas can make contradictory statements about the sanctions. One group can say that the sanctions are a failure because the Islamic Republic has not collapsed or agreed to Western demands about the nuclear program. Another can say that the sanctions are working because Iran's crude oil exports are down, its currency has lost value and it has difficulty accessing the international banking system. As long as the goal remains uncertain, all groups are perfectly correct in claiming success or failure.   ■

Policy options: few and bad

THE DESTRUCTIVE NATURE of U.S.-Iranian relations for over three decades leaves few attractive options for any U.S. administration. During that time Washington's complaints about Iran have remained constant: the Islamic Republic supports terrorism and terrorist groups, opposes the Middle East peace process, opposes American interests in the region, ignores its obligations under international agreements on nuclear weapons and has an appalling human rights record. Of course Tehran has its own list of grievances against the U.S. and the two sides—like a couple locked in a bad marriage—continue to remind themselves, the other side and anyone else who might listen, of their righteous indignation.

American policy options are few and all have costs. Those options are:

■ Military action (of an undefined nature), presumably targeting Iran's nuclear program. While the Obama administration insists that "all options (including this one) are on the table," it is clear that the U.S., after the difficult and costly experiences of Iraq and Afghanistan, has no desire to enter another conflict in the Middle East. Even the George W. Bush administration, with all its bluster, rejected this option.

■ Engaging Iran in order to begin a dialogue aimed at lowering tension and eventually resolving differences. As noted above, this path has proved extremely difficult and has encountered hostility, suspicion and old habits that will not change. These efforts

A million protesters took to the streets in Tehran to protest against the presidential victory of Mahmoud Ahmadinejad in what was the biggest demonstration yet since his declared victory, June 2009. (TEHRANREPORTER/DEMOTIX/CORBIS)

have always encountered setbacks and when they do both parties are ready to give up.

■ Covert action and sanctions against the Islamic Republic. While these actions avoid the negatives of direct military attack, their effectiveness is difficult to measure and their goal is uncertain. If too effective, such measures risk driving the Islamic Republic into a corner from which it could take reckless and dangerous countermeasures.

■ Encouraging Iran's democratic reformers. Again, the problem with this course of action is how to support which reformers. The American record in this area is disastrous. Reagan thought he was supporting anticommunist Iranian moderates in 1985; from time to time an Iranian dissident will attract some American backing until his supporters realize that he has a personal and financial agenda which has little to do with Iranian democracy. The 2009 pro-democracy "Green Movement" also attracted support from abroad, although its leaders had very problematic histories in the Islamic Republic. Some American politicians have gone so far as to support the MEK/MKO cultists, who are best described as promoting a combination of the Khmer Rouge murderous reign in Cambodia and the horrendous cult killing in Jonestown, Guyana.

Nor do conditions in Iran make for easy decisions in Washington. Those who made the Iranian revolution and have ruled the country since 1979 have made anti-Americanism a basic political tenet of the Islamic Republic. Although President Khatami attempted to undermine such thinking, he ultimately failed to make this important shift. At the same time, poorly understood factionalism in Iran has often paralyzed decisionmaking. Although precise information is difficult to find, it is clear that factions centered around powerful political figures are determined that no rival receives credit for anything. The recent (October 2012) fall of the Iranian currency has caused members of rival factions to put the blame on others for corruption, bad management and

KAL/CARTOONARTS INTERNATIONAL

economic illiteracy. When all else fails, one can always accuse rivals of being in the witting or unwitting employ of foreign powers.

Breaking the cycle

For all these reasons, both Iran and the U.S. have become mired in a pattern of suspicion, hostility and occasional violence. Attempts to change this pattern have run afoul of bad timing, toxic domestic politics, grievances real or imagined, and a deep reservoir of suspicion. When one side appears ready to move, the other side finds reasons to demur. It is also clear that, while this pattern serves the short-term interest of some politicians in both capitals, others on both sides recognize that there is a better and more positive path that will serve the interest of both sides—if only they could find a way onto that path.

Attempts to end this long estrangement have not fared well. Faced with failure and frustration, each side becomes confirmed in its prejudices and more strongly convinced that it is the reasonable one and that the "other" is simply too irrational, domineering, arrogant, duplicitous, etc. for any deal to be possible. Rather than persist in efforts to change a dangerous and self-defeating relationship, it is easier to throw up one's hands and say, "We were reasonable. But what can you do with such people?"

So what will work? From the frustrations and failures of 30 years, here

are some modest suggestions for a way forward:

■ Have patience and forbearance. Recognize that, with all the accumulated bitterness, progress will be slow and difficult. Expect frustration and do not give up at the first, second or third setback.

■ Have clear goals. What does the U.S. want from its relationship with Iran? What does Iran want? Strange as it seems, these goals have rarely been defined by either side.

■ Avoid gaming the Iranian system. Play the hand one is dealt. The time, the circumstances and the person will never be perfect. If one attempts to maneuver within a system one does not understand, the results can be disastrous.

■ Define progress realistically. The big breakthrough may never come and progress may be a small agreement or even something not said or not done.

■ Beware of the negative preconception. Assume failure—through a defect on the other side—and it will arrive. It will keep both sides captive to the destructive "rules" that have dominated Iranian-American relations for so long.

■ Be aware of the ghosts of history. When Iranians and Americans gather, there are always ghosts in the room. If we ignore them, they will haunt us anyway.   ■

✔ **Opinion Ballots**
after page 32

discussion questions

I. What stance has the Obama administration taken on Iran? How has the president moved past his predecessors, and in what ways has he failed to bring about better relations with Iran? How does cold-war logic continue to influence today's foreign policy?

2. Iran's growing nuclear program is viewed as a major threat to regional stability in the Middle East. What is the optimal U. S. response to Iran's nuclear program? How would a nuclear Iran affect American foreign policy? Have U.S. sanctions in Iran been effective? What purposes to these sanctions serve? Are they more harmful to ordinary Iranians or the regime?

3. How does the U. S. relationship with Israel affect its relationship with Iran? How far should U. S. support for Israel go? Do you think the U.S. should or should not have worked with Israel on covert actions such as cybersabotage of the Iranian nuclear program? If the U. S. decides to heed Israel's call and draw a "red line" for Iran's nuclear program, what would be the consequences?

4. What other countries should the U. S. rely on as it attempts to put diplomatic pressure on Iran? What role does the UN play in the Iran nuclear dispute? Is multilateral cooperation necessary? What other countries are concerned by the prospect of a nuclear Iran?

5. Discuss the history of foreign intervention in Iran. What was the historical context for each interaction? What were the results? How should this history inform foreign policy today?

6. What were the factors that contributed to the 1979 revolution? What significance does 1979 have today? Have the parties involved begun to move past its legacy? Is the anti-Americanism on display in Iran today based on current feelings, old rhetoric, or both? Are there hints that Iran is transitioning out of its 1979 mindset?

suggested readings

Abrahamian, Ervand, **A History of Modern Iran.** New York, Cambridge University Press, 2008. 228 pp. $28.99 (paper). Abrahamian provides a brief, readable, and scholarly account of 19th and 20th century Iran which examines the formative events of recent Iranian history.

Ansari, Ali A., **Confronting Iran.** New York, Basic Books, 2006. 280 pp. $26.00 (hardcover). Ansari, professor of modern history at St. Andrew's University, traces the course of American-Iranian relations going back to the early 20th century.

Bill, James A., **The Eagle and the Lion: The Tragedy of American-Iranian Relations.** New Haven, Yale University Press, 1988. 520 pp. $28.00 (paper). This is the best study in English of America's tangled relations with the Pahlavi regime. Bill, a professor of political science, is clear and unapologetic in his views, and outlines the scope of a great drama inhabited by numerous tragic heroes (and villains).

Cottam, Richard W., **Iran and the United States: A Cold War Case Study.** Pittsburgh, University of Pittsburgh Press, 1988. 298 pp. $25.95 (paper). Cottam, a political science professor and former official at the U.S. embassy in Tehran, lays out how Washington played the "great game" against the Soviet Union, with Iran as both prize and victim.

Limbert, John W., **Negotiating with Iran: Wrestling the Ghosts of History.** Washington, United States Institute of Peace Press, 2009. 215 pp. $16.95 (paper). This book contains four historical case studies of negotiation in which both Iran and the United States participated. From these studies the author extracts lessons which can help the American negotiator in understanding how to deal in an environment that has been very difficult for both sides for over 30 years.

Parsi, Trita, **A Single Roll of the Dice: Obama's Diplomacy with Iran.** New Haven, Yale University Press, 2012. 284 pp. $27.50 (hardcover). A readable and coherent account—largely based on interviews with participants—of how the Obama administration dealt with Iran policy.

Peterson, Scott, **Let the Swords Encircle Me.** New York, Simon and Schuster, 2010. 732 pp. $32.00 (hardcover). Peterson, the Istanbul bureau chief for *The Christian Science Monitor,* has an unerring eye for the martyrs, heroes, and opportunists who inhabit contemporary Iran. He is especially good at following how individuals lurch from one social and political extreme to another in reaction to disillusion and disappointment.

Slavin, Barbara, **Bitter Friends, Bosom Enemies: Iran, the U.S. and the Twisted Path to Confrontation.** New York, St. Martin's Press, 2007. 258 pp. $24.95 (hardcover). Slavin is a journalist who made numerous trips to Iran beginning in 1996. She has a special gift for going beyond high policy and capturing the essence of a brief encounters with ordinary Iranians.

Wright, Robin, ed., **The Iran Primer: Power, Politics, and U.S. Policy.** Washington, D.C., United States Institute of Peace Press, 2010. 268 pp. $24.95 (paper). This work is a collection of 50 brief articles covering topics including the opposition, the Iranian economy, the nuclear controversy, sanctions and U.S. policy from the time of President Carter.

China in Africa: Savior or self-interest?
by David Shinn

Chinese President Hu Jintao (c.), walks past delegates (from left to right, Cape Verde's Prime Minister Neves, Niger's President Issoufou, Equatorial Guinea's President Mbasogo and South African President Zuma) as he prepares to deliver an opening speech for the 5th Ministerial Conference of the Forum on China-Africa Cooperation held at the Great Hall of the People in Beijing, China, Thursday, July 19, 2012. (ANDY WONG/AP/CORBIS)

VISITORS to Africa in recent years almost certainly have been impressed by China's engagement. Today, China is deeply engaged almost everywhere on the continent, although four countries—Swaziland, Burkina Faso, São Tomé and Principe and Gambia—still recognize Taiwan. This is in stark contrast to the situation existing before the mid-1990's, when China was just one of many international actors on the continent. In 2009, China surpassed the U.S. as Africa's largest trading partner. It is important, however, to put this in perspective. Because China is such a major exporter and importer, trade with Africa constitutes only about 4 percent of its global trade. In contrast, China accounts for more than 13 percent of Africa's global trade.

China is also challenging Western countries in all areas of "soft power," such as student scholarships and specialized training in Chinese, technical assistance teams in Africa and the creation of a Chinese youth volunteer program in a number of African countries. It has expanded its radio, television and print media outreach to Africa and is establishing Confucius Institutes (cultural outposts of the Chinese government with some 350 branches on campuses around the world). China has some kind of military/security relationship with every African country that recognizes Beijing and now has about 1,500 peacekeepers assigned to six of Africa's seven United Nations peacekeeping missions. Since 2008, China has provided two frigates and a supply ship to the Somali an-

DAVID SHINN *is an adjunct professor in the Elliott School of International Affairs at George Washington University. He served for 37 years in the U.S. Foreign Service and is the former ambassador to Burkina Faso and Ethiopia. He is the co-author of* China and Africa: A Century of Engagement *and blogs at http://davidshinn.blogspot.com.*

Symbolizing China's eagerness to win new friends in Africa, Mao Zedong (r.) extends the hand of friendship to Ghana's President Kwame Nkrumah at a meeting in Hangchow, China., July 28, 1962. (BETTMANN/CORBIS)

tipiracy operation in the Gulf of Aden.

China has become a major force in Africa and has organized itself to remain for the long-term. There are areas where China and the West compete, such as trade, investment and commercial contracts, and there are other areas where interests overlap and China and the West could cooperate, such as UN peacekeeping, antipiracy initiatives, maintaining political stability and promoting economic development.

The future of competition and cooperation hinges on an obvious question: What are China's long-term interests? Does China only desire to extract oil and minerals to feed its industrial development? Or are other elements involved, such as developing another market for Chinese exports and maintaining the political support of African countries?

The dragon awakens in Africa

When the Communist Party of China (CPC) took control of the mainland in 1949, it was initially consumed with domestic issues and concerns on its immediate periphery. Africa was not important to its foreign policy interests. In any event, only Ethiopia, Liberia and white-ruled South Africa were independent, while Egypt had an element of self-rule.

China did not have good relations or, in the beginning, any relations with Africa's colonial rulers. As African countries began to achieve independence in the 1950s and especially in the 1960s, China realized that it needed their political support in the United Nations to replace Taiwan on the Security Council.

Beginning with the 1955 Asian-African Conference in Bandung, Indonesia, China worked hard to cultivate African delegations. China subsequently used conferences organized by the Afro-Asian People's Solidarity Organization to obtain support from the so-called nonaligned states. In 1956, China opened its first embassy in Africa in Cairo. Beijing's efforts paid off in 1971 when the UN General Assembly admitted the People's Republic of China (PRC) into the UN and also replaced Taiwan on the Security Council. The PRC obtained 34 percent of its votes from African countries; 26 African states supported Beijing and 15 backed Taipei, the Taiwanese capital. To this day, China regularly expresses appreciation to African countries for their support in gaining admittance to the UN.

Throughout the 1950's and 1960's, China backed African wars of national liberation, antiimperialism and antico-

lonialism. In the 1960's, China even supported a few left-wing movements that were trying to topple ideologically conservative governments. Increasingly, the Sino-Soviet conflict dictated Beijing's policy in Africa just as the cold war (1945–91) and anticommunism determined U.S. policy. China tended to support those liberation groups in countries still under colonial control that did not have Soviet backing and it made every effort to minimize Moscow's influence. This focus continued until the early 1980's when China and the Soviet Union reconciled. During the first four decades of its engagement with Africa, China had limited financial resources to devote to the continent and could not compete on equal terms with the Soviet Union or the West.

China's policy became increasingly pragmatic in the 1980s, but was also marked by an element of indifference, especially in the last half of the decade. China focused on internal economic modernization while the approaching end of the cold war reduced China's ardor for engaging in Africa. One of China's leading Africanists, He Wenping, said the guiding principle of Chinese diplomacy in the 1980s changed from "ideological idealism to pragmatic idealism and from unconditional internationalism to a priority of national interest." The decade ended with the government crackdown on the pro-democracy protests in Tiananmen Square in 1989, although this event did not adversely impact China's relations with African countries.

At the end of the cold war, decreased interest in Africa by the Soviet Union (now Russia) and the West coincided with the rapid growth of China's economy and its increasing need for raw materials. In 1993, China became a net importer of oil; Africa has about 10 percent of the world's known petroleum reserves. China's rapidly growing industrial sector also consumed increasing quantities of copper, bauxite, iron ore, cobalt, manganese, uranium, titanium and timber, all of which are found in abundance in Africa. By the mid-1990s, almost without notice, China had quietly begun to increase its engagement in Africa. ∎

China's interests in Africa

CHINA'S ENGAGEMENT in Africa, well-advanced by the beginning of the 21st century, had become so frenetic that in 2000 China created the Forum on China-Africa Cooperation (FOCAC), which meets every three years at the ministerial or summit level in an effort to coordinate China's relations with the 50 countries in Africa that recognize Beijing. In advance of the third FOCAC summit in 2006, China issued a major white paper on its African policy, which continues to guide the development of China's policy toward Africa. The fifth FOCAC ministerial meeting took place in Beijing in July 2012.

Although China is more economically advanced than every country in Africa, it continues to emphasize that it remains a developing country and, consequently, claims a special attachment to countries at a similar stage in Africa. While parts of China's interior still qualify as underdeveloped areas, the coastal region and even some interior centers such as Chongqing have clearly emerged from the developing category. It is doubtful that China will be able to claim for much longer that it is a developing country.

President Hu Jintao, speaking at the opening of the 2012 FOCAC ministerial meeting, emphasized his country's status as a "still-developing" country and said that China and Africa, as developing states, should align themselves more closely in global forums such as the United Nations. He then took a swipe at the West by adding: "We should oppose the practices of the big bullying the small, the strong domineering over the weak and rich oppressing the poor."

South African President Jacob Zuma, speaking after Hu, commented that "we certainly are convinced that China's intention is different to that of Europe, which to date continues to tend to influence African countries for their sole benefit." Zuma added, however, that Africa must be cautious and avoid allowing that sort of pattern to govern its relationship with China.

China currently has four hard interests in Africa. First, Africa is a source of raw materials. China obtains about one third of its oil imports from African countries and significant mineral resources: for example, about 90 percent of its cobalt, 35 percent of its manganese and 30 percent of its tantalum. It would be difficult for China to meet all of its mineral needs from non-African sources.

Second, China wants to expand its exports to Africa, which now has more than one billion people and a growing middle class, making the continent a more attractive export market. Between 2000 and 2010, China increased its exports to Africa thirteenfold.

Third, China seeks political support. African states now constitute more than one quarter of the membership of the United Nations General Assembly. China and many African countries that are criticized for their human rights practices tend to support each other in the United Nations Human Rights Council. China also welcomes African support in forums such as the World Trade Organization (WTO) and it, in turn, often supports African positions in the UN Security Council.

Fourth, one of Beijing's priorities is to end the diplomatic recognition of Taiwan by any country in Africa. Although only four African countries still recognize Taiwan, Beijing has never relented in its pursuit of the "one-China" policy. The 2008 election of Taiwanese President Ma Ying-jeou, who quickly developed a more cordial relationship with China, has resulted in an informal, but likely temporary, diplomatic truce between Beijing and Taipei. At some point, Beijing will almost certainly step up pressure on these four African governments to recognize China. At the same time, Beijing has no objection to Taiwan's commercial presence in Africa.

U.S interests in Africa

The U.S. has five hard interests in Africa. The first three are almost identical to China's. First, the U.S. seeks raw materials, especially oil. Although the U.S. buys more oil from Africa than does China, it imports fewer minerals and other raw materials.

Second, the U.S. wants to increase its exports to Africa, although they remain a tiny percentage of global American exports. Third, Washington tries to obtain support for U.S. positions in international forums from as many Afri-

Gold miners form a human chain while digging an open pit at the Chudja mine in the Ki-lomoto concession in north-eastern Congo, February 23, 2009. (FINBARR O'REILLY/REUTERS/ CORBIS)

can countries as possible. The only Chinese interest in Africa not shared by the U.S., for obvious reasons, is China's aim of ending diplomatic recognition of Taiwan.

The U.S. has two additional interests in Africa. First, the U.S. desires to minimize the impact in Africa of terrorism, narcotics trafficking, international crime, piracy and money laundering so they do not harm U.S. interests in Africa or at home. These concerns are not as significant to China as they are to the U.S.

Second, the U.S. military continues to rely on access to African ports for visits by naval vessels, on the ability to overfly African countries, and on the ability to land military aircraft at African airports. The U.S. has a military base in Djibouti and small drone intelligence-collection capabilities in Ethiopia and the Seychelles. It also operates small counterterrorism operations in Kenya, Uganda, South Sudan, Central African Republic and Burkina Faso.

So far, China has expressly denied it has any interest in establishing military bases or operations in Africa. However, as China expands its naval capacity, this could change.

State-to-state and party relations

The strength of China's relations with African countries lies in the state-to-state and party-to-party ties. China's official governmental relationships with each of the 50 countries in Africa that recognize Beijing is either excellent or, at least, satisfactory, and it works hard to maintain these cordial ties. The most telling fact is that every year since 1991 China's foreign minister has made his first overseas visit to a country in Africa. African leaders notice this consistency of attention.

High-level exchange visits with African counterparts permeate all layers of the Chinese government. President Hu has been to Africa six times, two as vice president and four as president. Between 1956 and 2006, some 160 Chinese leaders and foreign ministers visited Africa, while 524 Africans with the rank of minister or higher made 676 visits to China. These exchange visits have proved to be an effective and low-cost way to build a strong state-to-state relationship.

An especially important aspect of the official connection is the contact between the CPC leadership and African

ruling party counterparts in each country. Except for South Africa, where the Communist Party is a junior partner in the ruling coalition, none of the African ruling parties operates under the name of a communist party. Some of the ruling African political parties are ideologically close to the CPC but others have little in common with it. For example, Sudan's ruling party, the National Congress Party (NCP), professes to be an Islamic party. Yet the NCP and most ruling parties in Africa have established a close relationship with the CPC.

Between 1997 and 2006, the CPC hosted over 60 African party leaders. These visits permitted an exchange of views, coordination of policies, provision of modest financial assistance and even the voicing of grievances. The CPC has provided material support, for example, to the ruling political party in Zimbabwe. The CPC partners with like-minded ruling parties and offers cadre training and party management courses in countries such as South Africa, Tanzania and Namibia.

It is difficult to understate the importance of the CPC relationship with ruling parties in Africa, especially when comparing the situation to high-level U.S. contact with African leaders. Senior U.S. officials make fewer state visits to Africa and, excluding African attendance at the annual meeting of the UN General Assembly in New York, African leaders receive fewer invitations to come to the U.S. More importantly, the U.S. has nothing comparable to the CPC. The Democratic and Republican parties do not function as major decisionmaking bodies even when their leader occupies the White House. The only foreign engagement provided by the two major American political parties consists of low-level technical assistance and election monitoring by the National Democratic Institute and the International Republican Institute.

Military and security ties

Africa is of military and security interest to China only to the extent that there might be interruptions in access to and movement of oil and minerals that support Chinese industrial output.

Ivorian President Alassane Ouattara (r.) speaks with the Chinese ambassador to Côte d'Ivoire, (2nd l.), and the Ivorian Minister for Economic Infrastructure after the official launch of the jointly funded construction project of a 30 km highway linking Abidjan to Grand Bassam, on August 3, 2012. The infrastructure project is expected to cost $116.7 million. (SIA KAMBOU/AFP/GETTY IMAGES)

China prefers political stability in Africa and wants to minimize any threat to its personnel and interests there. China estimates that one million Chinese nationals now work and live in Africa, a number that is well above the figure for U.S. nationals. The death in 2007 of nine Chinese workers in Ethiopia's Ogaden region and the evacuation of 35,000 Chinese from Libya during the 2011 revolution were unpleasant surprises. China has not signed a formal military alliance with any African country. On the other hand, China has been a strong supporter of UN peacekeeping missions in Africa and the international effort to combat Somali piracy in the Gulf of Aden.

China's current policy emphasizes military operations other than war as a solution to international disputes. As in the case of its state-to-state contacts, China's military links with Africa rely heavily on a constant parade of Chinese military personnel visiting African counterparts and African military personnel hosted in China. The People's Liberation Army (PLA) coordinates its activities in Africa with the CPC and the state bureaucracy. PLA activities are political undertakings using military means for strategic reasons and not independent initiatives conducted explicitly for military purposes. At the end of 2007, China had 16 defense attaché offices in Africa, some accredited to multiple countries, while 28 African countries had comparable offices in Beijing as of 2010. The fact that China has relatively few defense attaché offices in Africa may reflect China's effort to downplay its military involvement.

Arms

China is a significant supplier of arms to Africa. From 2002 through 2009, China transferred (in most cases sold) $1.1 billion in conventional weapons to sub-Saharan Africa and another $1.4 billion to North Africa. The conventional weapons transferred to sub-Saharan Africa constituted about 20 percent of arms transferred by all suppliers. China helped Sudan to build its industry for assembling and producing small arms, artillery and armored vehicles. Nev-

Sailors from China's People's Liberation Army stand on the deck of a Chinese Task Force 525 flagship missile frigate that saw action in Somalia against pirates, as the ship anchored in Manila on April 13, 2010. (TED ALJIBE/AFP/GETTY IMAGES)

ertheless, China was a less important supplier by dollar value of conventional weapons to Africa than Russia or Germany. On the other hand, China is a more significant supplier of small arms, ammunition and light weapons, but there are no reliable statistics to document China's global percentage of these transfers.

Some of these weapons, especially small arms and light weapons, end up in African conflict zones. Together with arms from numerous other countries, they have been found in recent years in Sudan's war-wracked Darfur region, the brutal war in eastern Congo and anarchic Somalia. These weapons probably reached conflict areas after having been purchased on the international arms market or were transferred to groups involved in the conflict by compliant African governments that

Members of a special squad of the Chinese People's Liberation Army (PLA) Navy Seventh Escort Task Force participate in a joint drill with Tanzanian Marine Corps at a Navy base March 29, 2011, in Dar es Salaam, Tanzania. (XINHUA/GAMMA-RAPHO/GETTY IMAGES)

received them legally from China. The situation underscores, however, China's inability or unwillingness to monitor more effectively the movement of these weapons into conflict zones.

Military training is a growing component of China's cooperation with Africa. The PLA sends military experts to help with education, equipment maintenance and health care. China trains Zimbabwe's air defense personnel and pilots in connection with its equipment sales to the country and trained Equatorial Guinea's military in the use of heavy weapons. It has sent instructors to maintain military equipment in Sudan, Zimbabwe, Cameroon and Gabon. The PLA Navy held a joint training exercise with South Africa and conducted a military medical exercise in Gabon.

The most intriguing aspect of China's military connection with Africa is its current effort to expand the capability of the PLA Navy. While the western Indian Ocean is not an immediate priority for China, it is certainly part of the PLA Navy's long-term planning.

"China is interested in Africa's resources because they are interested in controlling their own economic destiny. And for China to control its own economic destiny, it must have a range of economic relationships and diplomatic partnerships that will allow them to procure sufficient raw material to keep the mother ship going."
—John Huntsman,
Former U.S.
Ambassador to China

www.GreatDecisions.org/DVD

Modern China made its first African port calls in 2000 with visits to Tanzania and South Africa. Following a hiatus, there has been an upsurge in port calls since China began sending ships to the antipiracy effort in the Gulf of Aden. This engagement has highlighted the difficulty of maintaining and supplying three navy vessels over an extended period of time without any permanent base rights in the region. As a result, China has been in discussions with Kenya and the Seychelles concerning the resupply of its ships. More importantly, China is well-advanced in building a nuclear submarine capacity and has begun to create an aircraft carrier task force. China currently must rely on the U.S. or Indian navies to protect the sea lanes that carry so much of its imported oil and minerals coming from Africa and the Persian Gulf. As PLA Navy vessels expand into the western Indian Ocean, they will bump up against both Indian and American naval ships and give rise to growing concerns about their objectives.

Trade, investment and aid

China's total trade with Africa grew from $6.3 billion in 1999 to $166 billion in 2011, a twenty-sixfold increase. When all 54 African countries are taken into account, trade over the years has generally been in balance, but there are huge disparities in bilateral trade. Some 15 African oil/mineral exporting countries tend to have large trade surpluses with China, while more than 30 others, generally the poorer ones, usually run large deficits. Trade for the remaining African countries is about in balance. Roughly three quarters of Africa's exports to China come from five oil/mineral exporting countries: Angola, South Africa, Sudan, Libya and the Republic of the Congo. In 2009, 80 percent of Africa's exports to China consisted of metals and petroleum products; other raw materials accounted for another 10 percent. To its credit, China is trying to increase imports from poorer African countries by allowing 4,700 items to enter duty free from Africa's least-developed countries. So far, this has not had a major impact on imports from those countries.

Most Chinese exports to Africa are high-value manufactured goods. Transportation equipment, machinery and electronic products account for half of its exports. China's exports are highly diversified, however, and include large quantities of textiles, footwear and plastic products. More than half of China's exports go to five countries: South Africa, Nigeria, Egypt, Liberia and Algeria. Increasingly, Chinese goods, especially low-end consumer products, are being sold by Chinese traders who have taken up residence in Africa and have an integrated supply system with friends and relatives in China. "Chinatowns" have appeared in cities such as Dakar (Senegal), Lagos (Nigeria) and Cape Town (South Africa). Some critics refer to China's trade and economic engagement in Africa as an example of neocolonialism. While there are certainly elements of mercantilism, the charge of neocolonialism misses the mark. China's trading practices are not significantly different than those of other major trading partners. Nor is there any effort by China to establish control over African governments.

Chinese investment in Africa only began in earnest in about 2000, long after companies from Europe and North America had entered the market. In recent years, Western investment in Africa has slowed considerably while Chinese investment has grown rapidly. Even using China's conservative figures, investment increased by more than 60 percent between 2009 and 2011. China has established a number of institutions to encourage overseas investment such as the China-Africa Development Fund and the China Export and Credit Insurance Corporation. Initial Chinese investment in Africa was concentrated in mining, energy, construction and manufacturing. Increasingly, China is moving into finance, aviation, agriculture and tourism. More than 2,000 Chinese companies, many of them small and private, have invested so far in Africa. South Africa, Nigeria, Zambia, Algeria, the Democratic Republic of the Congo and Sudan account for about 65 percent of China's investment in Africa. It is important to note, however, that this constitutes only about 4 percent of China's global investment.

Information on China's direct investment in Africa lacks transparency and is sometimes conflicting. As of the end of 2011, China stated its total direct investment in Africa had reached a cumulative $14.7 billion. The real figure is believed to be closer to $40 billion because of investments that go through locations such as Hong Kong and the Cayman Islands and are not included in the official total. It is probable that in the last several years China has been the largest bilateral investor in Africa, outpacing investment from the U.S. or any single country in Europe. Because companies in the U.S. and those in several major European countries started investing in Africa much earlier than China, their cumulative investments exceed China's.

China's minister of commerce, Chen Deming, asserted at the 2012 FO-CAC meeting that China will urge its companies and banks to participate in cross-border and regional infrastructure projects, encourage regional trade facilitation and eventually establish a comprehensive and diversified China-Africa trade and economic cooperation system. He said it is China's goal to migrate more production to Africa to create more jobs on the continent. Seven special economic zones now under construction in Zambia (two), Nigeria (two), Mauritius, Egypt and Ethiopia are intended to help achieve this goal. Chen added that China will request more investment protection and double taxation agreements. It will promote more experience and knowledge sharing with African counterparts in development concepts, policies, laws, regulations and industrial park development. Finally, Chen promised to encourage Chinese companies to fulfill their social responsibilities and pay greater attention to environmental concerns.

China is even less transparent about the level of its assistance to Africa and there is considerable confusion as to what constitutes aid as defined by the Organization for Economic Co-operation and Development (OECD). China

A Zambian worker digs a ditch in the Zambia-China Economic and Trade Cooperation Zone in Chambishi in the Copperbelt, the first zone of its kind in Africa. A Chinese worker is seen at the right, January 28, 2011. (THOMAS LEKFELDT/MOMENT/REDUX)

does not provide annual aid figures for individual countries. Specialists who have looked at this issue carefully suggest that in the past several years, China has provided about $2.5 billion annually in OECD-equivalent aid to Africa. This compares with about $8 billion from the U.S. The European Union (EU) provides even larger amounts. Although China is not yet in the top ranks of aid donors to Africa, it now provides enough assistance to qualify as a significant donor.

The component of Chinese assistance that is receiving the most publicity is the growing number of multibillion dollar soft loans for large infrastructure projects such as dams, railroads, roads, bridges, pipelines and buildings. The terms of these loans are usually better than similar commercial bank loans, but they usually do not qualify as OECD-equivalent loans. Except for China's insistence on recognizing Beijing rather than Taipei, there are no political strings attached to the loans, making them especially attractive to African governments that are wary of Western conditionality. On the other hand, these multibillion dollar loans are almost always tied to construction of the project by a Chinese company, often a large state-owned company, and sometimes include a significant percentage of Chinese labor. Nevertheless, China filled a void left by Western companies and is

now reaping an enormous amount of praise from African governments for meeting one of their priority needs.

While one can only guess at the value of China's development assistance, China's State Council reported in 2009 that almost 46 percent of its aid went to Africa, the largest regional recipient. Between 2000 and 2009, China also canceled $2.8 billion of debt owed by 35 African countries. There is no clear evidence that China is adding significantly to the debt of Africa's poorest countries. China is also increasingly engaged in multilateral aid organizations that tend to play an oversized role in Africa. It makes modest contributions to the United Nations Development Programme. Its voting share in the 188-member International Monetary Fund (IMF) has reached 6.1 percent compared to 16.5 percent for the U.S. and in the 187-member World Bank, whose mission is to help poor nations develop their economies, it is now at 4.42 percent compared to 15.85 percent for the U.S. China is also an active member of the African Development Bank and African Development Fund. The BRICS (Brazil, Russia, India, China and South Africa) are exploring the possibility of establishing a BRICS development bank to compete with the World Bank and other multilateral development banks. To the extent that China is willing to cooperate with

Is China an economic model for Africa?

There has been considerable discussion on the question of China as a development model for Africa. Often called the "Beijing Consensus" (as opposed to the "Washington Consensus") the argument is made, usually by African leaders, that their countries need to follow the economic success of China. Interestingly, China's officials have been careful to avoid pushing this idea. In fact, some have publicly warned that it would be inappropriate to emulate completely China's experience.

These cautions are grounded in several good reasons. First, there are just over one billion people in Africa's 54 countries compared to more than 1.3 billion in China. Nigeria, Africa's most populous nation, has about 160 million people. A number of African countries have populations of less than one million. The huge population difference calls into question the wisdom of trying to replicate China's development policy in any one country.

Moreover, China's success has been based on a high national savings rate, a large pool of cheap and compliant labor, state-targeted capital investments, a coherent continent-wide market with a single currency, internal market integration, a relatively well-educated and highly motivated workforce with a common language, invest-

ment from the Chinese diaspora, developed state institutions and political unity within a single ruling party. No country in Africa has even half of these attributes.

There is also a negative side to China's development: increasing income inequality between urban and rural areas, among regions and between the richest and poorest Chinese; growing pollution problems; and a willingness to sacrifice human rights and freedom of expression for the sake of national development. For that matter, there are different development models in effect across China itself. The rich coastal region operates on an industrial, export-dominated model, which is different from the economic model found in most of the interior. There are elements of Chinese development policy that might transfer successfully to some countries in Africa. One of them, the special economic zones, is already being established, as discussed earlier.

China's success at poverty reduction is another program that may have positive lessons for Africa. There may also be some useful borrowing from China's educational and agricultural policies. But the idea of transplanting China's development model to any particular country in Africa is just fantasy. ∎

other donors, it prefers to do so within the context of the UN system, where it has growing influence, rather than the Western-dominated OECD's Development Assistance Committee.

China constantly reminds other donors that it does not attach political strings to its assistance, and this is generally true. On the other hand, should any African leader publicly criticize China's internal policies on issues such as Tibet or the treatment of Uighur Muslims in western China, the impact on China's aid to that country should be observed. There is no criticism either because African leaders agree with Chinese policies or because they do not want to risk a rebuke. In any event, African leaders prefer not to deal with political conditionality that is often imposed by Western countries. As one Chinese official told the author several years ago, "No African leader has ever asked us to attach conditions to our aid." While China may not attach political strings, World Bank economist Ali Zafar concluded that China uses aid "principally to facilitate trade and

improve access to natural resources."

President Hu announced at the 2012 FOCAC ministerial meeting that China will provide $20 billion in credits to Africa over the next three years. This is double the pledge made at the 2009 FOCAC. He said the loans would support infrastructure, agriculture and the development of small businesses. Although he did not offer details of the loan terms, they probably are similar to previous loans based on attractive commercial terms with repayment in most cases made by the shipment of raw materials. In the case of infrastructure projects, Chinese companies will certainly obtain the contracts and there will likely be a percentage of Chinese labor. China also announced at the 2012 FOCAC that it will promote its currency, the renmimbi, for settling trade and investment deals in Africa and encourage more countries to use it as a reserve currency. The Bank of Ghana has already taken this step.

Other soft power

Although the official numbers tend to go up and down depending on who makes

the announcement, Hu Jintao commented at the 2012 FOCAC that China has trained about 40,000 African personnel in a variety of sectors and provided more than 20,000 government scholarships to students from African countries. The scholarship figure actually seems low inasmuch as China announced more than a year ago it is offering 5,000 scholarships annually. In any event, China is making a major government effort to attract African students. The U.S. no longer offers a comparable program except for the small Fulbright Program, started in 1946 to increase "mutual understanding," although many African students come to the U.S. at their own expense or are sponsored by universities. China and countries in Africa have paired 20 universities as part of a project to link institutions of higher learning. China has also established 29 Confucius Institutes in 22 African countries. Most of them are at African universities where the institutes offer Chinese language, culture and history.

Since 1963, 18,000 Chinese medical personnel have served in 46 African countries. China claims these teams have since the beginning of the program treated 200 million patients. In 2005, China began sending small numbers of young volunteers organized by the CPC Youth League. Between 2009 and 2012, more than 350 volunteers worked in African countries, most of them in health, medicine, education and technical fields. Although the program is tiny compared to the U.S. Peace Corps program in Africa, it is one more example of China's desire to engage at all levels of soft power.

Xinhua, China's official news organization has more than 20 bureaus in Africa and regional centers in Cairo and Nairobi. It competes with Reuters, Agence France Presse and Bloomberg, and in some countries in Africa it is the only international news service. Xinhua produces both public news and "internal reference" reports for the Chinese government. Xinhua reporters work closely with counterparts in African governments' official news agencies. As a result, they are often among the best-connected and informed reporters. China Radio International (CRI) launched its first overseas-based FM radio station in Kenya in 2006 and now has offices in Cairo (Egypt), Lagos (Nigeria), Nairobi (Kenya) and Harare (Zimbabwe). It broadcasts and hosts Web sites in Arabic, Hausa, Swahili, English and Chinese. China Central Television established a station in Nairobi at the beginning of 2012. China also announced in 2012 its intention to create a China-Africa Press Exchange Center in China to increase interaction between the correspondents of media organizations from both sides. ∎

Challenges for China in Africa

CHINA HAS MUCH working in its favor, but it faces some serious challenges. While China has developed especially good relations with African governments, it has done rather poorly with African civil society, opposition political parties and independent labor unions. This comes as no surprise. Civil society is weak in China. Because there are no opposition political parties and no independent labor unions, China does not understand how to deal with these components of society. On the other hand, China has generally been successful in interacting with the African commercial sector, including private companies.

Democracy and human rights

The approach to African countries by the U.S. and China about democratization and human rights practices constitutes the most important difference in their respective African policies. It is China's policy to eschew political conditionality such as putting pressure on countries to improve human rights practices and to democratize. Most African governments welcome China's policy.

The U.S., on the other hand, sees this as a major part of its interaction with Africa. Autocratic African governments disdain this approach while democratic countries such as Botswana and Mauritius are more receptive. Even the democratic states, however, are sensitive to political conditionality. So long as the U.S. makes this an important policy consideration, China will have an advantage in working with most African governments.

Where there is a strong civil society, these groups often deplore China's willingness to ignore human rights abuses and even prop up undemocratic regimes. African opposition political parties also feel ignored by China, although on those rare occasions when they overturn ruling parties they are usually quick to improve relations with Beijing because they welcome China's investment capital.

Strong labor unions in the few African countries where they exist, such as South Africa and Nigeria, have been especially critical of China's impact on Africa. Textile imports from Asia, including China, decimated about one third of Africa's production several years ago. Labor unions, not always accurately, put the blame on Asian imports.

Chinese imports

Africa is being flooded with inexpensive Chinese products and increasingly Chinese traders are displacing African merchants in the marketplace. Most

A Nigerian salesman of soccer balls made in China tosses one up into the air in an outdoor market in Cotonou, Benin. Chinese exports to Africa enter markets here and then go on to west Africa. February 13, 2008. (JEAN CLAUDE MOSCHETTI/REA/REDUX)

Chinese employees work at the Nile Textile Group factory in the free zone of Port Said, Egypt, on November 8, 2009. With cheap labor, investment incentives and unrestricted exports, one Chinese textile group has turned to Egypt as an ideal location to produce its ready-made garments, beating stiff competition at home. (KHALED DESOUKI/AFP/ GETTY IMAGES)

African consumers welcome the availability of Chinese products, although there are complaints about low quality, because they are usually cheaper than comparable products made in Africa.

Cheap Chinese imports make it difficult, however, for African manufacturers to turn a profit or, in some cases,

Members and supporters of the Kwazulu-Natal Christian Council and Diakonia Council of Churches held a morning prayer, "Arm-in arm against arms" on Durban's beachfront on April 19, 2008 to protest against the offloading of arms from China destined for poverty stricken Zimbabwe. International sanctions imposed by Western countries against Zimbabwe include a ban on weapon sales to the country. (RAJESH JANTILAL/AFP/GETTY IMAGES)

even remain in business. In addition, private Chinese traders with their integrated supply chains and willingness to work longer hours are displacing African counterparts, especially in west and southern Africa. This has resulted in growing public criticism of Chinese traders and created, in some cases, a public relations nightmare for China.

The media

The collaboration between government-controlled media organizations in Africa and counterpart organizations in China has been noted. The downside of this arrangement is China's tendency to isolate the growing number of private sector media organizations in Africa. Some Africans are beginning to express concern about the motives of China's engagement in this sector. Private Kenyan media companies were displeased, for example, when a Chinese company received the contract to distribute media content digitally. They perceived the deal as giving China an opportunity to interfere in Kenya's press freedom, as this does not exist in China.

Arms transfers

China is a major supplier of small arms and light weapons to Africa. Some of these weapons end up in conflict zones. It is China's policy to keep them out, but their widespread availability guarantees that some get in. China has not shown much interest in monitoring these transfers and has not taken steps proactively to prevent their movement into African conflicts.

Western critics have expressed concern that China's multibillion-dollar loans to African countries may add excessively to African debt and undercut efforts by the West, the World Bank and the IMF to encourage good governance. While they do serve as a disincentive to improving governance, there is no solid evidence they are leading to excessive debt. Most of the loans go to resource rich countries that can afford to pay down the loans by shipping raw materials to China. They may be a problem, however, for countries without natural resources.

Labor

Some Chinese companies have a poor record on worker safety and following local labor laws. A case in point was Chinese involvement in Zambian copper mines, where an explosion killed a number of workers and labor conflict has plagued the operation. In 2011, the opposition party even won the election in part by running on an anti-China platform. Once in power, however, the new government, after realizing the magnitude of China's investment in Zambia, quickly restored good relations.

Other issues that have confronted China in Africa are the selling of counterfeit and adulterated products. In the case of textiles based on African designs, manufactured in China and then resold in Africa with Made-in-Africa labels, the situation is only embarrassing. In the case of medicines that may not have the indicated amount of active ingredient, the product is dangerous. China is trying to stop these practices, but it is difficult to monitor the private sector and African countries are ill-equipped to identify the fake and adulterated products. China has also been criticized for some of its environmental practices in Africa. Again, it recognizes the problem and is trying to do better.

U.S. policy options

Africa is essentially neutral territory for both the U.S. and China. While the U.S. has traditionally been more engaged in Africa in the post-World War II era than China, Beijing has come on strong in the 21st century and has surpassed the role of the U.S. in some countries and in some areas, such as trade. Both countries intend to remain engaged in Africa for the long-term. It was only about six years ago that the U.S. began to take seriously China's growing role in Africa. The options for U.S. policy in dealing with China are limited by global economic concerns and increasing restrictions on the international affairs budget. In addition, the issue is much more complicated than just China in Africa. A number of emerging nations such as India, Brazil, Turkey and Indonesia—and returning ones such as Russia—are joining the rush to Africa. It is hard to deal with competition from China in isolation.

The U.S. does not have the financial resources or the political will to counter China at every level of its engagement in Africa. In fact, such a policy would result in an unnecessary waste of scarce U.S. resources and probably achieve limited success. Nor does abdication of influence to China make much sense. Even with its diminished budgets, the U.S. still brings considerable resources to the table. Its aid to Africa is much higher than China's; its cumulative private investment is greater than China's, although the PRC's private and state-owned industry investment is growing faster. America's military reach is much longer than China's. Those African countries truly interested in establishing democratic governance will continue to look to the West and the U.S., not China, for moral and political support.

The preferred option for the U.S. is to compete in some areas and seek cooperation in others. Obvious areas for competition are in the export and contract sectors where companies from both countries routinely vie for business. China has been winning this competition easily over the past decade. It has some advantages in that many of its deals are packages involving government financing and political back-

Sudan's leader Omar al-Bashir (r.) and Chinese President Hu Jintao (l.) review a Chinese military honor guard during a welcoming ceremony at the Great Hall of the People in Beijing on June 29, 2011. (LIU JIN/AFP/GETTY IMAGES)

ing combined with the sale of Chinese products or bidding on large contracts by Chinese private and state-owned companies. Private American companies generally operate independently and are especially handicapped because there is much less U.S. Export-Import Bank financing (which helps sell American goods overseas) available, American companies must find ways to become more competitive and convince Congress to provide more government financing.

There will also be a continuing competition for serving as the example of the best way to govern a country. African governments see the advantages and disadvantages of the systems in the U.S. and China and rarely want to emulate one or the other in its entirety. But those governments that lean toward Western style liberal democracy, free and fair elections, a free press, an independent judiciary and the ability to express views openly find themselves in tune with the U.S. Others tend to follow the Chinese system.

The policy opportunity that has received the least attention in the U.S., China and Africa is the chance for China and the U.S. (and perhaps others) to cooperate to the mutual advantage of African states. The obvious areas where there already has been some cooperation include providing funding and personnel for UN and the 54-member

African Union (AU) peacekeeping operations in Africa, the antipiracy effort in the Gulf of Aden, policy coordination in response to African conflicts in areas such as Sudan/South Sudan and Somalia and the search for political stability generally in Africa. This cooperation should continue.

There could be much more collaboration in the area of development assistance. Both countries have major programs for combating malaria that would benefit from greater cooperation. China and the U.S. could pool their respective strengths in efforts to improve pandemic preparedness and to reduce neglected tropical diseases such as hookworm and schistosomiasis. Both countries also have significant experience in aiding African agriculture, which consumes the labor of 60 percent of the African labor force but is still not able to grow enough food to feed its people.

Some African governments seem to be preoccupied with the idea that it is in their interest for China and the U.S. to compete in Africa. This is valid in the case of trade, investment and bidding on commercial contracts. It does not apply, however, to efforts to further develop Africa and prevent disease. ■

✔ **Opinion Ballots**
after page 32

discussion questions

1. Why does China have a long-term interest in Africa? Is it only a desire to extract oil and minerals to keep its industry producing at a high level? Will Africa ever become a major market for Chinese exports? Now that China is a global power, does it really need to pay so much attention to the political support of African countries? What are the potential implications of natural resource extraction on the environment?

2. Some writers and even U.S. policy officials have described China's engagement in Africa as an example of neo-colonialism. Is this a valid criticism? Why or why not?

3. Mercantilism is also a frequent charge leveled against China's policy in Africa. What is it? Is it appropriate to describe China's policy as one of mercantilism? Why or why not?

4. So far, China has not been a positive influence on improving human rights practices and encouraging democracy in Africa. Do you think this will continue to be the situation in the coming decades? Are there ways to encourage China to play a more positive role in this area? Are there ways that the U.S., working with African leaders, can move China more positively in this direction?

5. Should the U.S. be concerned about China's military buildup, especially its plans to expand the navy? If the PLA Navy becomes a frequent visitor to the western Indian Ocean, will this pose a threat to American security interests in the region? What should the U.S. do about it? Are there potential areas for U.S.-China naval collaboration in the western Indian Ocean?

6. What are the prospects of U.S.-China cooperation in Africa? There continues to be considerable criticism of China in the American press, among the public and on Capitol Hill. Will this skepticism prevent the U.S. from collaborating with China in Africa assuming the Chinese and Africans are even interested in such collaboration?

7. Do you agree with the author's assessment that, taken in its totality China does not serve as an appropriate economic model for Africa? If you disagree, what are the arguments put forth by some African leaders that China is the best model? In the final analysis, is the Beijing Consensus about as meaningless as the Washington Consensus?

suggested readings

Brautigam, Deborah, **The Dragon's Gift: The Real Story of China in Africa**. New York, Oxford University Press, 2009. 397 pp. $21.95 (paper). Drawing on three decades of experience, Brautigam emphasizes the role of China's aid, trade and investment in Africa.

Shinn, David H. and Eisenman, Joshua, **China and Africa: A Century of Engagement.** Philadelphia, University of Pennsylvania Press, 2012. 524 pp. $69.95 (hardcover). This is a baseline study of China and Africa that looks at all aspects of the relationship over the past century. It includes four regional chapters that cover China's bilateral relations with each country in Africa from the date of diplomatic recognition to the present.

Taylor, Ian, **China's New Role in Africa.** Boulder, Lynne Rienner Publishers, 2009. 226 pp. $24.00 (paper). Taylor argues that Beijing is using Africa not only as a source of raw materials and potential new markets but also to bolster its own position on the international stage. He traces the history of Sino-African relations and looks at key issues such as oil diplomacy, trade, human rights, arms trade and peacekeeping.

For more news and analysis, we recommend the following Internet resources:

African Economic Research Consortium, <www.aercafrica.org/publications/all.asp>. This website contains a 54 page list of monographs dealing with economic issues in Africa, all free of charge. There are numerous academic papers on China-Africa topics included among them.

Forum on China Africa Cooperation, <www.focac.org/eng>. This is China's official website for the Forum on China Africa Cooperation. It contains the key documents and speeches for the five ministerial and summit conferences that have been held so far. It also provides from China's perspective additional background information on its relations with Africa.

South African Institute of International Affairs (SAIIA), <www.saiia.org.za/occasional-papers/blog.html>. This website contains a long list of occasional papers of 20 to 30 pages each on a variety of topics dealing with China in Africa. It also has shorter policy briefings on China-Africa issues.

Stellenbosch University, Centre for Chinese Studies (CCS), <www.ccs.org.za>. This website contains monographs on China-Africa relations, a monthly newsletter called China Monitor and a weekly briefing on China-Africa issues.

TO LEARN MORE ABOUT THIS TOPIC AND TO ACCESS WEB LINKS TO RESOURCES GO TO www.greatdecisions.org

Assessing threats to the U.S.
by Gregory F. Treverton

Workers disinfect the waiting room of a Beijing railway station in the fight against SARS, May 25, 2003. (PETER PARKS/AFP/GETTY IMAGES)

WHAT, IF ANYTHING, puts the American way of life at risk? The advisory board of RAND's Center for Global Risk and Security has ranked threats in three categories—existential, serious and inconvenient. The board judged that at present the only threat that qualifies as existential—that is, could put at risk the American way of life—is a major pandemic.

If Americans needed a reminder that the economy is critical, the last five years have provided that in spades. There is no "national security" issue more urgent than getting a grip on the U.S. fiscal imbalance lest markets and foreigners draw their own conclusions. That risk, if not threat, of economic collapse is probably not existential but could come close.

China is serious as both a threat and opportunity. It remains a policy challenge of the sort the U.S. has not seen recently—a possible military competitor that is also a critical economic partner. The Arab Spring and its aftermath also rank in the serious category, and also pose both threats and opportunities. Dealing with one nuclear rogue, North Korea,

is in the inconvenient category but the other, Iran, ranks as serious. Finally, cyberthreats may be serious but still are not well calibrated.

What did not make this list? Three threats are worth mentioning. One, terrorism, probably ranks between inconvenient and serious. Soon after Sept. 11, 2001, when the concern about the terrorist threat bordered on hysteria, the chair of the center's board, former Secretary of Defense Harold Brown, was asked how he would rank the threat on a scale of one to ten, with ten the worst. His answer: if the Cuban missile crisis of 1962 was an "eight," terrorism is a "three." The answer was a surprise then but has turned out to be right,

GREGORY F. TREVERTON *directs the RAND Corporation's Center for Global Risk and Security. He has worked on the staff of the first Senate Select Committee on Intelligence and the National Security Council staff, and he was vice chair of the National Intelligence Council. His latest book on intelligence is* Intelligence for an Age of Terror *(Cambridge, 2009).*

Investigators and emergency personnel at the scene after Congresswoman Gabrielle Giffords and 13 others were wounded, and six people were killed, when a gunman opened fire during a meet-and-greet event outside a grocery store in Casas Adobes, Arizona, January 8, 2011. (JAMES F. PALKA/ZUMA PRESS/CORBIS)

Third, while the globalized world is blurring "domestic" and "foreign," one threat—internal violence in the U.S.—is very domestic in its roots and implications. Historically, most terrorism in the U.S. has been domestic. Indeed, if anything is surprising, it is that there has not been more violence already, though the shooting of Representative Gabrielle Giffords (D-Ariz.) in January 2011 sadly testifies to the possibility. The ingredients are all there: a deeply polarized nation awash in guns and ammunition; the Web as reinforcement for like-minded extremists; prisons as hotbeds of radicalization; and a black president as symbol. Violence seems more likely from the radical right, though those groups are well penetrated by the Federal Bureau of Investigation and closely monitored by private watchdogs like the Southern Poverty Law Center. It is also too easy to imagine interactions of right and left: imagine a counterprotest to 2011's Occupy Wall St. movement. ■

in part because the U.S. and its partners have acted to prevent terrorist attacks.

A second threat, climate change, probably will be an inconvenience for the U.S., at least until some tipping point sets off dramatic change, like the melting of the Antarctic ice shelf. Any threats to the U.S. will be mostly indirect, for instance the ripples of Africans driven by water or food shortage to migrate where they are unwanted, touching off internal conflict.

Pandemic threat

IN ADDITION TO being ranked in severity from inconvenient to existential, threats might be characterized across a continuum. At one end are purposive threateners who mean us harm, like terrorists. At the other end are what might

Vials containing 10 doses of Swine flu vaccine are shown here September 29, 1976, in Pennsylvania, prior to being shipped out as part of massive nation-wide inoculation program. (BETTMANN/CORBIS)

be labeled "threats," like global warming, that simply result from individuals acting in their own interest. The people who release carbon into the atmosphere mean no harm; in that sense, if the product of their actions can be regarded as threats, they are "threats without threateners." Organized crime is somewhere between a purposive threat and one without threateners. That is so because the violence and lawlessness of organized crime can become a threat worthy of being called one to security even though the main purpose of the criminals is only to enrich themselves, not harm innocents.

Pandemics are special because they might be either a threat without a threatener or a purposive threat (from a terrorist group, for instance). That is the reason for the dotted line in figure 1. The rub is that it would probably not be clear for some time whether the pandemic derived from a purposive threat. However, the upside of that downside is

that preparations for a pandemic inflicted by "Mother Nature" should also be helpful in the case of a purposive threat.

Pandemics are the classic low-probability-but-high-consequence event that policymakers find so hard to address. That difficulty was vivid in policymaking toward a possible "swine flu" pandemic in 1976. The strain, the same virus believed to be the agent of the 1918–19 global flu pandemic in which 500,000 Americans died, appeared when a U.S. Army recruit collapsed and died during a forced march at Fort Dix, New Jersey. Scientists and doctors at the Centers for Disease Control and Prevention (CDC) erred on the side of professional caution and said simply that they could not quantify the probability of a pandemic. In fact, many of the doctors privately thought the probability was low. But what policymakers heard was different. One common description of the threat was "a very real possibility," and one policy official said, "The chances seemed to be one in two that swine flu would come." So an unknown probability had become an even chance. What ensued was an ill-fated effort to vaccinate the entire nation.

If a pandemic becomes real, it will almost certainly be a zoonotic virus—a pathogen that emerges from an animal to infect, and spread among, human beings. Influenzas are zoonoses, emerging from wild aquatic birds and sometimes using a pig as an intermediary host on the way to humanity. AIDS is a zoonosis, and so is ebola. SARS is a zoonosis that emerged from a Chinese bat. By contrast, hantaviruses, like those that killed tourists at Yosemite last summer, emerge from animals—common deer mice were the hosts of the Yosemite virus—but cannot be transmitted from human to human. While they are untreatable and very lethal—perhaps approaching 40 percent— any infection of a human from the dust of dried mouse urine or feces produces a dead-end host, alas perhaps literally so for that human host.

The next pandemic threat will not be a hantavirus, nor is it likely to be ebola, which not only can be stopped by eliminating direct contact with the bodily fluids of those infected but also proves fatal so quickly that its victims are not good candidates for global transmission. Only one person has been known to leave Africa with a rampant ebola infection.

Since any pandemic is likely to be a threat without a threatener, there is great incentive for nations to cooperate in responding. And, indeed, international cooperation has been increasing. As the instance of SARS demonstrated, once the disease was identified, every medical person in the world became a collector of intelligence on the outbreak. SARS spread from Guangdong province in southern China, and within a matter of weeks in 2002 and early 2003 had reached 37 countries around the world. More than three months passed from the first information about the disease to a global alert. It was then another month until the virus was clearly identified. The time delay may have had something to do with China's dissembling about the extent of the disease, but

Purposive Threats and "Threats without Threateners"

PURPOSIVE THREATS **RANGE OF INTENT** "THREATS WITHOUT THREATENERS"

ORGANIZED CRIME

DRUG TRAFFICKERS

CLIMATE CHANGE

TERRORISTS

PANDEMICS

INCREASING RISK OF LETHALITY

SOURCE:
Threats Without Threateners, Gregory F. Treverton, Erik Nemeth and Sinduja Srinivasan. RAND Corporation, 2012.

it also demonstrates that the cause of any outbreak—whether natural or terrorist—may take some time to identify.

SARS led to 8,096 known infected cases and 774 confirmed human deaths. This resulted in an overall case-to-fatality rate of 9.6 percent, which leapt to 50 percent for those over 65. By comparison, the case-fatality rate for seasonal influenza is usually less than 1 percent and primarily among the el-

derly, but can rise many-fold in locally severe epidemics of new strains. The 2009 H1N1 virus, which was estimated to kill about 18,000 people worldwide, had a case-fatality rate no more than .03 percent in richer countries. Thus, in the two recent major disease outbreaks, SARS and H1N1, the world had the good luck to "practice" cooperation on viruses that either were not very contagious or very lethal. ■

With protective masks covering their faces, staff at the ticket counter of the Lima, Peru, international airport assist travelers, May 21, 2009. The airport required employees to wear the masks to prevent the spread of the H1N1 flu virus. (XINHUA/EYEVINE/REDUX)

8

Looming economic crisis

IF THIS IS A THREAT, and it is, it is not a threat without a threatener. Unfortunately, as Walt Kelly's comic-strip character, Pogo, put it: "We have met the enemy and he is us." The mood in the U.S. remains strikingly insular. The 2012 elections were almost entirely devoid of foreign policy but for grace notes—nostalgia for American greatness, along with promises to restore it, and some discussion of how much to spend on defense. In one sense, the insularity is on the mark because America's role in the world will turn on how it handles—or does not handle—its fiscal situation.

The recovery from the crisis of 2007 to 2009 has been very slow, which is also a cautionary note about America's ability—and, perhaps more important, will—to play a major global role in the decade ahead. The bottom line is that the U.S. economy would have to grow at an annual rate of 7.6 percent in 2012 to catch up to the average recovery; in fact, most projections are in the range of 2 percent.

The immediate issue is sequestration as required by the bipartisan Budget Control Act (BCA) that Congress approved in August 2011, after a "supercommittee" charged with agreeing on a major budget deal came to gridlock. The BCA is supposed to trigger automatic cuts totaling $1.2 trillion, evenly split between defense and nondefense discretionary spending. A $487 billion reduction in defense spending is already before Congress in the budget for fiscal year 2013, but that is a reduction in planned defense spending increases over the next 10 years. Unless Congress acts, the BCA requires that the next $500 billion cut would take effect in January 2013, as required under the BCA, as part of a broader, 10-year, across-the-board reduction. Thus, the immediate future will be a game of chicken involving Congress and the executive over the federal budget, including entitlements and defense.

The sad irony of the gridlock is that, in economic terms, neither the fiscal problem nor the pain required to fix it is all that severe. Nor is the need for cutting imminent. Indeed, given the slow recovery, there was and is a strong argument for economic stimulus beyond what the Federal Reserve can supply. Yet given the Republicans' success in framing the issue as government spending out of control, there is not much chance that President Barack Obama would propose or that Congress would support further fiscal stimulus in the form of deficit spending. What the country requires is a plan for addressing the deficit, not immediately but when the economic recovery reaches some threshold.

The National Commission on Fiscal Responsibility and Reform plan announced at the end of 2010 is not a bad place to start. It called for $1 trillion in additional revenue, about $2.2 trillion in spending reductions, and about $700 billion in interest savings over 10 years, phased in over time to avoid pushing the economy into recession. If the task is not hard economically, however, it seems virtually impossible politically. The commission's report, often labeled "Simpson-Bowles" after its bipartisan cochairs (Republican Alan K. Simpson and Democrat Erskine B. Bowles), seemed dead on arrival in Washington. The Commission needed 14 votes of 18 members to formally approve the report but only got 11. Republicans broadly rejected the report, and President Obama did not embrace it.

Much of the rhetoric about U.S. debt has been overheated. For all its fiscal problems, the U.S. has remained a relatively safe haven in a stormy world economy, and so U.S. interest rates, far from soaring, are at or near all-time lows. Inflation is tame, and the dollar has not plunged in value. Rather, the real foreign policy concern is what fiscal retrenchment will mean for U.S. engagement abroad. In the best of worlds, a soft retrenchment will impose painful choices, including in defense and foreign policy. The worse risk is that that other nations could decide that the U.S. lacked the willingness or ability to get its fiscal house in order. Then a falling dollar might coincide with a major sell-off of Treasury securities, which would then reverberate through

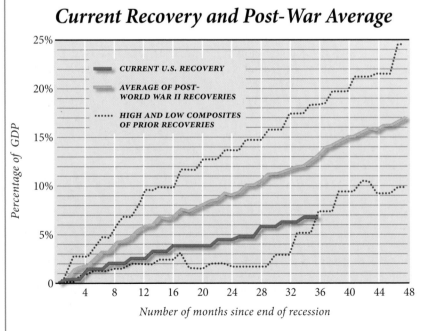

Current Recovery and Post-War Average

CURRENT U.S. RECOVERY

AVERAGE OF POST-WORLD WAR II RECOVERIES

HIGH AND LOW COMPOSITES OF PRIOR RECOVERIES

Percentage of GDP

Number of months since end of recession

SOURCE: Council on Foreign Relations; Bureau of Economic Analysis

other markets. In those circumstances, the U.S. would confront truly unattractive choices—dramatically cut spending quickly, or drive up interest rates to protect the dollar, thus plunging the economic into recession—a vicious cycle of economic and political decline: witness Japan, which feels to sophisticated observers as though it, while still rich, has become rather uninterested in the wider world.

Europe's crisis is intertwined with America's, and it also contains some cautionary lessons for the U.S. The structural problems with the economic and monetary union (EMU) and the creation of the euro in the Stability and Growth Pact of 1997 were visible from the start. The basic problem was that a common currency requires a common fiscal policy, and the 27-member European Union (EU) does not have one. Some crisis was virtually inevitable even if predicting its shape and timing was elusive. In the U.S., because the federal government takes a substantial share of taxes and provides a similar share of transfer payments, when recession hits a U.S. region—during the oil crisis recession, for instance, or the high-tech bust—the effect is cushioned because tax payments from that region go down and transfers to it rise. By contrast, that "fiscal federalism" is very limited in Europe because the EU takes only a sliver of Europe's income in taxes, and virtually all of that goes to support agriculture and subsidize the poorer regions.

Will the euro zone survive intact? Only time will tell. Germany has moved grudgingly to accept the logical solution to the immediate crisis—turning national debts into euro-zone debt—but even that will not eliminate the underlying structural problem. Meanwhile, non-euro-zone member Britain embarked on just the regime of immediate spending cutting that is widely advocated for the U.S., only to see its economy fall back toward recession, with predictions of no growth for 2012. Britain's folly underscores that what the U.S. needs is a plan to rein in the deficit but *not* immediate measures to do so. ∎

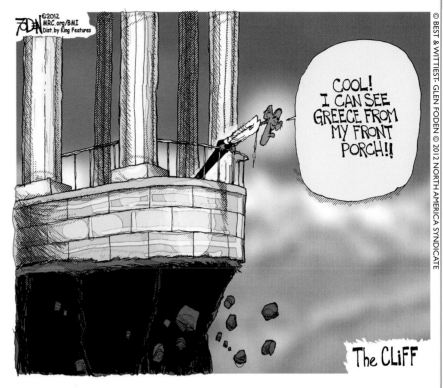

The CLiFF

Asian challenge, China puzzle

The facts of Asia's emergence—actually reemergence in historical perspective—are well known. China is of course the lead. Its economic transformation is without historical parallel. It has grown faster, longer than any state in history—over 9 percent annually for 30 years. It lifted 400 million people out of poverty in a generation. Indeed, the lion's share of the poverty reduction on the planet over that period is attributable to China. Even as China's growth slows, China will continue to make a rising contribution to global, growth. That is because China in now a tenth of the global economy, two and a half times what it was in 2001.

Asia's rise is often thought of, mistakenly, as a "transfer of wealth"; rather it is a transfer of power driven by a growth of wealth in Asia. Asia, and especially China, will continue to grow in importance to the U.S. That is reflected throughout society, from the faces on U.S. college campuses to the fact that more than half of Silicon Valley start-ups are led by immigrants, most of them from Asia. However this growing importance is labeled, it carries policy implications for the U.S. The rise of China, then India, is producing a much more multilateral system, one in which more states have more vested interests in the stability of the international system, hence enlarging the range of possible partners for U.S. action.

America, in turn, will be able to strategically share leadership with other nations and lessen its burden, or shape more efficient coalitions—by first approaching democracies with common values and then "selectively engaging" countries with a true stake on a given issue. But those new partners will also demand a real voice, and they will occasionally act on their perceived interests in ways that annoy the U.S., so patience in following long-run interests through short-term perturbations will be required.

China presents a unique policy challenge—a country that is simulta-

Anti-Japan protesters hold portraits of the late Communist leader Mao Zedong, Chinese national flags, and a poster that reads: September 18, National Humiliation Day, while marching on a street outside the Japanese Embassy in Beijing September 18, 2012. (ALEXANDER F.YUAN/AP/CORBIS)

neously a potential military foe and a critical economic partner. For that reason, conversations about China in Washington and Los Angeles seem not to have the same country as their subject: they are dominated by peer competitor in Washington but by economic opportunity in Los Angeles. Perhaps the last such challenge was pre-World War II Germany, but it was much less important economically, and it fairly quickly resolved into a military foe. China and the U.S. are locked in an economic version of the 1945–91 cold war's nuclear "mutual assured destruction" between the U.S. and the Soviet Union: either country could do enormous damage to the other but only at the price of taking itself down as well. For instance, China is the largest single holder of U.S. government debt, with about 8 percent of $16 trillion as of autumn 2012. If China tried to sell that debt off rapidly, it could do considerable damage to the U.S. but only at the price of dramatically driving down the value for itself of the debt holdings.

China's defense capacity has grown rapidly as its economy has boomed, though it remains focused on its periphery, as the sparring with Japan over disputed islands has indicated. Sino-American armed conflict is hardly inevitable, and is probably not likely given the shared economic stakes. Yet there is no shortage of issues which carry the risk of accident or miscalculation. Taiwan is most often cited, but Korean scenarios, especially the collapse of North Korea, may be somewhat more likely. Cyberconflict could seem to require physical retaliation, and as the islands suggest, saber-rattling in the East or South China Sea could lead to more than rattling. And conflict with regional rival India remains a possibility, if perhaps at the bottom of this list of probabilities.

It almost goes without saying that any of these conflicts would confront the U.S. with very unpleasant choices. Currently, U.S. capabilities would allow for a direct defense in most of these contingencies, with chances of success high in the South China Sea, medium in Korea and somewhat less in Taiwan. Over time, though, as China's capabilities improve, U.S. choices will shift to escalation—with the hope that the threat will deter China—and remaining aloof from the conflict.

The years ahead promise to compound the China puzzle. It has long been assumed that, sooner or later, growth would slow and that the social change driven by economic growth would lead to political change. Now, there is a good argument, though hardly proof, that the timing is "sooner." Demographics is one powerful driver. China will soon fall off the demographic cliff, as the fruits of the one-child policy mean a rapidly aging population. And, critically, China will begin to age when it is still, relatively, poor, and thus is not like aging in Japan or Europe.

Moreover, for both economic growth and political change, the key indicator is when China will reach a per capita income of $17,000 per year in 2005 purchasing power parity. This benchmark will be passed in 2015 if China continues to grow at 9–10 percent annually, or in 2017 if growth slows to 7 percent. Correlations are not predictions, but no non-oil rich country with a per capita income over that level is ranked as other than "free" or "partly free" by Freedom House, though China remains firmly "non-free." As China has gotten richer, its people have become less inhibited in raising their voices, and the Internet provides them increasing opportunities, notwithstanding the government's zeal in censoring it. The government has stopped enumerating what it calls "mass incidents"—strikes or protests usually carefully crafted to stick to local issues—but an estimate for 2010 puts them at 160,000, up from 10,000 in 1995. Another indicator is the visible nervousness of China's leaders about the polity over which they rule.

On the economic side, one recent study found that high growth in non-oil exporting countries ended at a per capita income of about $17,000. There are good economic arguments for the threshold: the payoff from shifting workers from agriculture to industry diminishes, as does the benefit from adapting foreign-developed technologies, and an undervalued exchange rate also is a factor. In this study, growth slowed from 5.6 to 2.1 percent per year. A drop of that magnitude in China's growth would take it to the 6–7 percent range. Again, there is nothing magic about correlation, and China might escape the threshold by developing its own internal undeveloped "country" in western China. Moreover, much of the world would be delighted with 6 percent growth.

Yet economics and politics will intersect. If growth slowed, what sectors and what people would be hit? How much would unemployment and underemployment increase, including for college graduates? Slowed growth would have some effect on China's armament and on its ability more generally to use money as soft power. The order of the shocks would also matter. If some political liberalization came first, that might cushion the effect of the economic slowdown. If the order were the reverse, that might set off some political opening. Or it might lead to a period of heavy-handed repression. In any case, China—and Asia—will remain a preoccupation for the U.S. ∎

The Arab Spring and its discontents

Who would have thought a match struck in December 2010 on a forlorn street corner in Sidi Bouzid, Tunisia, by a street vendor drenched in paint thinner would ignite the entire Middle East? The region, like China, represents both threat and opportunity, and qualifies as "serious" in the rankings because it touches so many interests of the U.S., from oil to Islam to Israel. This ignition of what came to be called, perhaps now with some irony, "the Arab Spring" was a beginning but hardly an end. Turmoil continues: witness the killing of U.S. Ambassador Christopher Stevens in Libya in September 2012, in a terrorist plan amidst regional anger at a viral video defaming the Prophet Muhammad done by an obscure Coptic reactionary living in Los Angeles. The bloody stalemate in Syria has claimed as many as 40,000 lives. Beyond Syria, the new complication is natural gas, which is itself an opportunity but one that will put further pressure on relations between Israel and Turkey, and the issues involve the intersection of regions and factors—in particular, Middle East politics, energy and the Arab Spring.

While democracy has been on the march since the 1970s, the Arab world had not joined the march. So at least the uprisings of the Arab Spring put the lie to easy Western stereotypes of docile Arabs cowering before corrupt strongmen. Yet while the 1979 Iranian revolution is ancient history, it still hangs over the region—and American policy. What was striking then was how eager the revolutionaries were to topple the shah, assuming that what would follow would be a secular social democracy. Instead, it was the mullahs who captured the revolution. Now the concern is that radical Islamists of different stripes, better organized and more ruthless, will reap the fruits of the Arab Spring. According to one expert, more than half the 30-odd Syrian opposition groups are radical Islamist. In general, the Arab Spring has been hard on religious minorities across the region, as well as on the rights of women.

Radical Islamists come in many sizes and shapes, and it would be a mistake to lump them too easily together. One common inspiration for many of the groups, especially those labeled Salafis, is Wahhabism, a fundamentalist strain of of Sunni Islam centered in Saudi Arabia. To be sure, not all radicals are Salafis, just as not all Salafis, or Saudis, are Wahhabis. Yet virtually all Salafis are Wahhabis. The concern is that, just as Wahhabi money funded South Asian madrasas that provided the foot soldiers for Afghanistan's Taliban 30 years ago, this time around Wahhabis will try to capture the "spring" by helping the Salafis who have been given new opportunities by the political openings in many Arab countries.

The Arab Spring will play out in different ways in different countries, but four factors bear watching. Perhaps most important is the interplay of Islamist and more secular parties. In Egypt, the governing Muslim Brotherhood so far has walked a delicate line—Islamist enough to remain credible to hard-core supporters but tolerant enough to sustain relations with the U.S. and Israel. In effect, for all the apparent tension between the Brotherhood and

People attend a campaign event for Egypt's Salafist al-Nour party prior to parliamentary elections in the Giza neighborhood in Cairo, Egypt, December 6, 2011. (SHAWN BALDWIN/CORBIS)

the military, the military sought stability and turned to the group most organized to produce it, the Muslim Brotherhood.

The second factor to watch is the role of the military. More plural politics, not to mention democracy, cannot ensue without civilian control of the military, which was entrenched in many Arab countries and engaged in lucrative business ventures. Again, Egypt is a vivid example. When Egyptian soldiers were killed in the Sinai Peninsula in August 2012, the episode was a humiliation for the military and especially for its leadership, the Supreme Council of the Armed Forces (SCAF). Mohamed Morsi took advantage of the episode to cashier a clutch of senior military leaders. At the same time and on his own, he amended the March 2011 constitution declaration to give his office executive and legislative powers. At one stroke, in effect, he unilaterally imposed civilian leadership with hardly a whimper of protest from the military.

A third factor is building new institutions. Arab countries transitioning from highly personalistic regimes will confront considerable state-building challenges. Countries transitioning from strong institutionalized authoritarian systems will require the type of thorough institutional reform that was needed during democratization in Eastern Europe. Yet, other countries have overcome the sectarian or other social divides that bedevil the Arab world. Moreover, successes in producing more plural politics often look inevitable in hindsight but were far from given at the time. Portugal, for instance, had six provisional governments in the first 27 months of its transition, and it experienced mass purges and a transitional military government riven by ideological differences.

The fourth factor is economic. On many indices of state failure, some sharp break in some Arab country was predictable well before the Arab Spring. What was not easy to predict was when and where, or precisely how. Those same indices will hang over the future, in particular the "youth bulges," especially of young men, many of them unemployed and perhaps unemployable. The same dissatisfaction with economic conditions that helped drive regime changes poses a challenge in the aftermath. For instance, the greatest risk to a successful opening in Tunisia may be that a period of economic hardship could tempt its citizens to renew the old bargain that exchanged political rights for economic benefits. Tunisia is more dependent than other Arab states on tourism, so it also confronts the risk that internal violence will drive away foreign visitors. ■

Dealing with nuclear rogues

The U.S. grudgingly accepted both India and Pakistan as nuclear weapons states after their nuclear tests in 1998. A decade later, the U.S. embraced India in the 2008 U.S.-India Nuclear Cooperation Approval and Non-proliferation Enhancement Act, which made India the first nuclear weapons state that is not a party to the 1968 Nuclear Non-Proliferation Treaty (NPT) regime but is still permitted to conduct nuclear commerce with the rest of the world. The convoluted language of the act's name reflected the U.S. dilemma: on the one hand, India's nuclear weapons status was not going to be reversed, and making real the enduring rhetoric of cooperation between "the world's two largest democracies" was tempting. Yet on the other hand, the agreement was one more nail in the coffin of the NPT regime—the principal international instrument for containing the spread of nuclear weapons.

With India and Pakistan accepted into the nuclear club, the immediate challenge for non-proliferation effort comes from the two nuclear rogues, Iran and North Korea. The first qualifies as a "serious" threat because of the effect a nuclear Iran might have on its neighborhood. North Korean is less threatening than Iran, more in the inconvenience category, because it is a weaker and more isolated power. Whether the Iranian nuclear weapons program can be kept in remission through a "grand bargain" between Iran and the U.S. has been an issue at the top of the Obama administration's agenda. If a deal that includes putting the Iranian fissile material production infrastructure under tight International Atomic Energy Agency (IAEA) inspection does not materialize, then Iran could build the capacity to enrich enough uranium to create a bomb by no later than the middle of the next decade. The region would face, if not an actual a "Persian/Shi'a bomb"—indeed in 2012 U.S. intelligence continued to hold the view that the Iranians had made no political decision to build a weapon—then at least an Iranian "nuclear option," one that could be exercised quickly.

Israel, which has managed an impressive 40-year nuclear monopoly in the region with its undeclared but fully hinted nuclear arsenal, regards an Iranian bomb as an existential threat. In the circumstances of enrichment capacity but no consensus that Iran has decided to build a weapon, the possibility of a military strike on Iran's nuclear facilities has provoked open discord between the Obama administration and the Israeli government of Benjamin Netanyahu. In September 2012, Netanyahu talked of the world but meant the U.S.: "The international community is not setting Iran a clear red line, and Iran does not see international determination to stop its nuclear project," he told his cabinet. "Until Iran sees a clear red line and such determination, it will not stop the progress of its nuclear project—and Iran must not be allowed to have nuclear weapons."

Beyond the immediate wrangling was the question of whether a strike could really retard Iran's nuclear march, given the dispersion of its facilities and the hardening of some of them in underground installations. The U.S. position was that the military option could delay but not destroy Iran's nuclear program. In any case, it was plain that an air strike big enough to do serious damage was at the limit of Israel's capacity—and perhaps beyond it without American help, at least in aerial refueling.

U.S. policy sought both to pressure Iran and to reassure, hence restrain, Israel. The administration organized major international military exercises in the region in September, sought to build a regional missile defense system, and began to talk more about what has been called "Olympic Games," the covert cyberattacks begun in President George W. Bush's administration and accelerated by Mr. Obama. Those attacks infected Iran's nuclear centrifuges and sent them spinning out of control before Iran discovered the attack in 2010. Meanwhile, the administration argued that the continued tightening of sanctions against Iran, particularly those that affect its oil exports, were having an effect.

A nuclear Iran would raise the concern that several Sunni-dominated states, such as Saudi Arabia, Egypt and Turkey, will find this new status quo intolerable. Given the close political military ties between Saudi Arabia and Pakistan, the former might acquire both an operational arsenal and delivery systems from the latter. Egypt and Turkey may well attempt to follow Iran by first building up a civilian nuclear power infrastructure and then using that mobilization base to move on to a nuclear weapons program.

If the other rogue, North Korea, is more an inconvenience than a serious threat, still, a final resolution of North Korea's nuclear status through the demise of the NPT regime would be a very hard landing for the region. Over a generation, the U.S. and its allies have tried everything from sanctions to relative generosity. The Clinton administration seriously contemplated war in 1994, but finally opted, instead, for the Agreed Framework to freeze North Korea's nuclear activities, carrots instead of sticks. It agreed to provide North Korea with fuel, normalized relations and, ultimately, nuclear power plants

North Korean military officers at the Pyongyang Indoor Stadium celebrate on May 26, 2009, one day after North Korea staged an underground nuclear test, the country's second successful nuclear test. (KNS/AFP/GETTY IMAGES)

if North Korea abandoned its nuclear weapons efforts.

The framework broke down as both sides alleged the other had reneged, and North Korea withdrew from the NPT in 2003. It announced a successful nuclear test in 2006 and apparently conducted another in 2009. During this time, the U.S. and allies have sought to engage North Korea in the "six party" talks— the two Koreas, U.S., Japan, China and Russia, occasionally supplemented by

bilateral U.S.-North Korea discussions, even as the allies apply sanctions. China is regarded as the only power with much influence in North Korea; not only is how much unclear, but China appears ambivalent, not wanting a nuclear North Korea but also fearing instability on its borders. The only safe bet seems that this unlikely "mouse," a near failed state, North Korea, will continue to roar loudly enough to preoccupy the U.S. and its Asian allies. ■

Cyberthreats still uncalibrated

THE CYBERTHREAT surely is inconvenient, and it could be serious. It is hard to know which because the threat remains uncalibrated. The Pentagon has suffered "peacetime" cyberspace attacks from parties known and unknown. Yet the threat goes well beyond the military to the pillars of society itself, for the infrastructures usually taken for granted—from information, to finance, to transport, to water—all depend on cyberspace. Most of this infrastructure is in private hands, not public. Estimates of the damage from *today's* cyberattacks within the U.S. range from

hundreds of billions of dollars to just a few billion dollars per year. Most of U.S. commerce and finance treats the threat as an inconvenience. It has been able to absorb the losses and prefers to accept that inconvenience rather than impose inconvenience on its customers. Biometrics, redundancy and other measures could make cyber commerce much safer, but so far, apparently, major companies have not reckoned that the benefits justified the costs—or the inconvenience.

The lack of calibration both grows from and complicates the divides over

"There's an old adage that this war is not like the last war. This war is not like the next war. This war is like this war. The point being that they're all different. The enemy has a brain; the enemy adapts and adjusts to whatever the United States does."

—Donald Rumsfeld,
Former Secretary of Defense

www.GreatDecisions.org/DVD

which cyber policy must be made—public-private, civil-military, offense-defense, public-private—and which have bedeviled the making of policy. The first divide, public interest but private ownership of infrastructure, was underscored by the fate of regulatory legislation in 2012. Sponsored by Senator Joseph Lieberman (I-Conn.), the bill would have empowered the Department of Homeland Security to set security standards for important national infrastructure in private hands. The legislation foundered when those owners argued that the standards would impose costs on them. Given the impasse, the debate turned to an executive order, not a law. But, even with an executive order, legislation would still be needed to provide liability protections for companies that share threat information with the federal government, increasing criminal penalties for cybercrimes and enhancing cybersecurity personnel, hiring authorities and salaries.

The second divide, civil versus military, has been demonstrated by the difficulty in filling the position of civilian czar for cyber policy, a position announced with great fanfare in May 2009. Alas, in official Washington the label "czar" usually connotes major

responsibility but minor authority and few troops. The country seems to be moving, for want of better, toward vesting responsibility not just for the government's cyber safety but also for the country's, in military institutions, especially the National Security Agency (NSA) and the Cyber Command, whose commander is dual-hatted as the director of NSA. Many leaders in information technology had spent their careers trying to get government off their back, so when Google turned to NSA in 2010 for help with its China problem, the nation perhaps had crossed a threshold.

The divide between offense and defense confounds assessments of the threat. The two are organizationally separate in the U.S. government. Offense, in particular, is so highly classified that those who work on defense know little of it. This means that "red-teaming"—running the best U.S. offenses against U.S. defenses—does not occur. To pose threats, adversaries need a combination of access, tools and intelligence. In particular, the threat requires not just penetrating the system but understanding how it works. In that sense, such "red-team" exercises as have been conducted, and which have often produced what appear to be serious breaches in cyber systems, may be

artificial, since by definition the opponent begins with an understanding of how U.S. systems operate.

Returning to basic principles helps to parse the threat and guide policy. It is tempting to seek analogies between cyberwar and cyber deterrence, on one hand, and nuclear war and nuclear deterrence on the other. Yet the two realms are quite different. Attributing attacks was less of a challenge in the nuclear realm; any major attack would have had an address. Not so for a cyberattack, which could be mounted through computers hijacked around the world. Nor is it obvious that successful attribution would drive policy options. Any nuclear attack would have been horrific enough so that threatening retaliation in kind was credible enough. Threatening physical retaliation for cyberattack may be both incredible and unwise.

Nuclear attack could impose strategic damage; it was a truly existential threat. By comparison, there seems little possibility of *strategic* cyberwar. Each attack points out vulnerabilities to the party that is attacked, and most of the damage can be fixed relatively quickly. For those reasons, the emphasis in cyber policy is on robustness, defense and repair, not deterrence or threats of retaliation. ∎

Framing policy options

The only existential threat, pandemics, probably does not require new policy initiatives beyond the steady building of international surveillance and response networks. If American politicians and pundits have hyped the terrorist threat, one beneficial side effect has been the beefing up of state and local first-response capabilities, ones needed for pandemics and natural disasters as well as terrorist attacks.

Fiscal Policy

President Obama's new administration will confront two immediate sets of decisions in January 2013. The over-

arching one is putting America's fiscal house in order. The challenge, once the immediate crisis is past, will be to build, first, an argument for fiscal discipline rooted in national security and, second, ways to take and enforce the required—and painful but not too painful—choices. Achieving fiscal discipline will require new revenue sources, such as a value-added tax, and special procedures, such as fast-track authority for approving trade agreements or the procedures for military base closing and realignment, that amount to some tying of the hands of the executive or Congress, or both, once some blue-ribbon panel has reached recommendations. There seems little stomach in the body politic for any of these remedies.

Syria

The other immediate decision point is the Middle East. Should the U.S. intervene militarily in some fashion to oust the regime of Bashar al-Assad and stop the killing? The options range from providing weapons to the opposition forces, to establishing a no-fly zone, to sending special forces to neutralize Syria's unconventional weapons, especially chemical weapons, to direct intervention. The Obama administration has confined itself to humanitarian assistance to opposition forces, arguing that providing weapons would only increase the killing and that Russia and China will block any United Nations Security Council sanctioning of force, without which no U.S. ally will join Washington.

Iran

Here, the issue is whether to continue to play for time, hoping sanctions will have an effect. Surely, they have begun to bite, as Iran's currency devalued dramatically in the fall of 2012. The risk, as in other sanctions cases, is that sanctions will give the regime just the foreign devil it needs to buttress its support at home. Iran's nuclear facilities are far more extensive than Iraq's (or Syria's), so a small strike would have little effect. The military challenges are daunting, including, in the words of one comprehensive analysis: "overflight of Arab territory, the distances Israeli aircraft would have to fly in penetrating Iranian airspace, finding ways to refuel and support enabling aircraft in hostile air space, range-payload problems in penetrating deeply into Iran, the risk of losing aircraft to fuel problems if they had to make combat maneuvers, and the ability to do lasting damage to Iranian hard targets like Fordow and Natanz." Without American help, the best estimate is that Israel could delay Iran by a year or two.

The Arab Spring

Beyond Syria, the U.S. will be deeply affected by how the Arab Spring plays

Detail of the National Debt Clock, a billboard-size digital display showing the increasing U.S. debt, near an office of the Internal Revenue Service on Sixth Avenue, July 26, 2011, in New York. (STAN HONDA/AFP/GETTY IMAGES)

out but have only limited ability to influence events. Perhaps the best policy guide are the words of Hippocrates: "do no harm." Patience, that most un-American of traits, probably will be required in, for instance, not quickly withdrawing U.S. aid to Egypt over its misbehavior, or in recognizing that inviting Islamists into the political process can build stability, or that asserting civilian control over the military, not to mention creating new institutions, will take time. Postponing justice for former dictators may also be necessary.

China

Here, continuity is the default policy. The Obama administration wisely dropped the language of a "pivot" toward Asia, which seemed to gratuitously insult those from whom policy was pivoting (Iraq and Afghanistan) and worry those toward whom it was pivoting (China and Asia). That U.S. attentions, including military, will naturally shift toward Asia only makes sense; giving that shift an emotive label does not. Given the risks of miscalculation, caution is called for. So is restraint in responding to economic issues, like perceived unfair trade practices or overvaluation of Chinese currency.

Nassim Nicholas Taleb, an options trader turned philosopher (of *Black Swan* fame), makes an intriguing point about fragility, one that has implications for foreign policy. The opposite of fragile is not, he says, robust; rather it is anti-fragile, meaning that the object (or policy) positively benefits from being bounced around. Of course, just as nothing is purely fragile, so, too, nothing is purely anti-fragile. Good companies may be anti-fragile across some range, with minor crises making them better but big shocks putting them out of business. For foreign policy, robust is probably the best that can be hoped for: notice how fragile U.S. policy was in the Middle East when the Arab Spring dawned. Given the uncertainties there, as well as in China, fashioning policy that is robust through the expected unexpected is the challenge. The other implication from fragility is the human tendency to "fix" problems much as we fix broken plates—by restoring the *status quo ante*. That temptation too was evident in the American response to the Arab Spring. It blinds policy to new possibilities. At least the Arab Spring made clear there is no going back. The future will be different from the past, and the challenge is to find opportunities in that future. ∎

✔ **Opinion Ballots**
after page 32

discussion questions

1. Do you agree with the author's classification of threats as existential, serious and inconvenient? Is the United States safer now than in years past? Which threats have increased and diminished in seriousness?

2. Why has U. S. economic recovery following the 2008 financial crisis and the recession been slower than past recoveries? What will be the short and long term effects if the BCA's automatic cuts are allowed to take effect? Is more economic stimulus the solution? How should the deficit be addressed? How can the economy be viewed as a national security issue?

3. Discuss how China represents a unique challenge and opportunity for the United States. How should the U. S. balance China's economic benefits with its status as a potential military foe? Will China's role on the world stage be affected by its demographic and political difficulties? Discuss the implications of the "pivot to Asia" in U.S. security strategy. Why might tensions rise between the U.S. and China?

4. Do you agree with the author's contention that terrorism should not be viewed as a significant threat to the U.S.? How might new Islamist regimes influence U.S. policy about the Middle East?

5. Discuss the so-called "Nuclear Proliferation Treaty regime." How do Iran and North Korea each put pressure on the NPT regime with their rogue nuclear programs? Is the Nuclear Proliferation Treaty irrelevant today? If so, why? What framework, if any, might take its place? What other strategies can be used in dealing with rogue nuclear states?

6. As cyberattacks become more prevalent on the global stage, how should the U.S. protect itself? How should the public sector, including companies such as Google and Twitter, interact with the private sector to address this threat? Is cyberwarfare a new national security concern? How is it like or unlike past threats to U.S. security?

suggested readings

Brzezinski, Zbigniew, Brent Scowcroft, and David Ignatius, **America and the World: Conversations on the Future of American Foreign Policy.** New York, Basic Books, 2008. 304 pp. $16.95 (paper). This book is a comprehensive look at current American foreign policy, written as a series of dialogues between Brzezinski (a professor at Johns Hopkins University) and Scowcroft (former National Security Adviser to both Gerald Ford and George H. W. Bush). The book puts special emphasis on China and the Middle East.

Dobbins, James, David C. Gompert, David A. Shlapak, and Andrew Scobell, **Conflict with China: Prospects, Consequences and Strategies for Deterrence.** Santa Monica, The RAND Corporation, 2011. 24 pp. $10.00 (paper). Available online at: <http://www.rand.org/pubs/occasional_papers/OP344.html>. This occasional paper was prepared for the U. S. military and details hypothetical scenarios that could lead to military conflict with China within the next 30 years.

Libicki, Martin C., **Cyberdeterrence and Cyberwar.** Santa Monica, RAND Corporation, 2009. 238 pp. Available free online at <http://www.rand.org/pubs/monographs/MG877>. Libicki presents an analysis of cyberwar and speculates on the future of cyber attacks. He also outlines ways that countries can protect themselves in the face of cyberwarfare.

National Commission on Fiscal Responsibility and Reform, **The Moment of Truth.** December 2010. Available free online at <http://www.fiscalcommission.gov/sites/fiscalcommission.gov/files/documents/TheMomentofTruth12_1_2010.pdf>. This is the full Simpson-Bowles commission report, which presents solutions for U.S. economic recovery. The plan was not formally approved by Congress.

Pollack, Jonathan D., "The United States, North Korea, and the End of the Agreed Framework." **Naval War College Review** 56 (2003). 11–49. This paper provides a general background on the Agreed Framework adopted by the Clinton administration in its dealings with North Korea, as well as an overview of the framework's disintegration.

Treverton, Gregory F., **Intelligence for an Age of Terror.** New York, Cambridge University Press, 2009. 320 pp. $40.00 (hardcover). This book focuses on how the analysis of terrorism has changed during the 20th century. It also contains a deeper explanation of the concept of a threat without a threatener.

Underwriting lifelong relationships.

We are Starr Companies, a global insurance organization supporting those who not only dare to reach for the farthest shores, but thrive when they get there. That is why, from the East Coast to the Far East, our exceptional teams set new standards for risk management across a broad spectrum of industries. Because we seek out the bold ones. The visionaries. The dreamers and doers. And when we find them, we don't merely stand by their side. We put our name in ink, below theirs, as they venture forth to explore, discover and achieve the amazing. Starr Companies: **Underwriting the future.**

STARR
COMPANIES
GLOBAL INSURANCE & INVESTMENTS

starrcompanies.com

Accident & Health ✦ Aviation & Aerospace ✦ Casualty ✦ Construction ✦ Crisis Management ✦ Energy ✦ Environmental
Financial Lines ✦ Marine ✦ Professional Liability ✦ Property ✦ Public Entity ✦ Specialty Products ✦ Travel Assistance

TOPIC 1: MIDDLE EAST

ISSUE A. The U.S. is on the "right side" of the new governments and movements that have been borne from the upheaval in the Middle East.

Strongly agree	5%
Agree	63%
Disagree	29%
Strongly disagree	3%

ISSUE B. The NATO mission in Libya was championed and led by Britain and France rather than the U.S. In future international interventions, the U.S. should take a backseat role with limited participation.

Yes	64%
No, the U.S. should take a leading role	11%
No, the U.S. should not participate in such efforts at all	5%
Other	20%

ISSUE C. The U.S. should reassess its relationships with semidemocratic allies such as Saudi Arabia and Bahrain.

Strongly agree	20%
Agree	63%
Disagree	14%
Strongly disagree	1%

ISSUE D. The regime changes in Egypt, Tunisia and Libya have left al-Qaeda on the sidelines and demonstrate that the organization has fallen in public opinion in the Arab world.

Yes	35%
No	21%
Not sure	45%

TOPIC 2: PROMOTING DEMOCRACY

ISSUE A. Any U.S. efforts at democracy promotion should be channeled through organizations like NATO and the UN, rather than undertaken unilaterally.

Strongly agree	28%
Agree	46%
Disagree	23%
Strongly disagree	4%

ISSUE B. The United States should actively promote democracy around the globe.

Strongly agree	13%
Agree	59%
Disagree	25%
Strongly disagree	4%

ISSUE C. In your opinion, which method of promoting democracy is the most appropriate unilateral U.S. strategy?

Diplomacy	41%
Sanctions (includes conditional aid)	8%
Democracy assistance in the form of funding, training, organizing, etc.	51%
Military force	1%

ISSUE D. The U.S. should be more accountable to domestic constituents about the disbursement of democracy assistance.

Yes	70%
No	10%
Not sure	21%

TOPIC 3: MEXICO

ISSUE A. Should the U.S. pursue anti-drug initiatives in Mexican territory without explicit permission from the Mexican government?

Strongly agree	5%
Agree	15%
Disagree	51%
Strongly disagree	29%

ISSUE B. Who should lead efforts to combat drug cartels and criminality in North and Central America?

U.S. alone	1%
Mexico alone	1%
U.S. and Mexico	58%
Central American nations	6%
Mexico and Central American nations	34%

ISSUE C. The Obama Administration should restore the ban on semi-automatic weapons that lapsed in 2004.

Yes	85%
No	9%
Not sure	6%

ISSUE D. In your opinion, how should the U.S. government prioritize the "Four Pillars" of the Mérida Initiative? (Rank 1=Most important and 4=Least important)

	1	2	3	4
Provide equipment, technology and training to disrupt the capacity of organized crime.	24%	35%	29%	12%
Professionalize the military and police and improve the judicial system.	23%	29%	33%	16%
Enhance border security to curtail illicit transborder movement.	22%	14%	20%	44%
Create jobs and pursue social initiatives, such as youth programs, to create drug-resistant communities.	39%	22%	15%	25%

TOPIC 4: CYBERSECURITY

ISSUE A. In cases like the London riots of 2011, governments have a "law and order" interest in controlling cyberspace.

Strongly agree	21%
Agree	56%
Disagree	19%
Strongly disagree	4%

ISSUE B. What party or parties is best equipped to lead in the global governance of cyberspace?

A multilateral body, like the UN, where all countries have a say.	28%
Liberal democracies, such as the U.S., that have a commitment to open networks.	14%
A collaboration between the public and private sectors.	55%
The private sector alone.	3%

ISSUE C. The U.S. government should actively promote the openness of networks in authoritarian countries where content is filtered.

Yes	65%
No	12%
Not sure	23%

ISSUE D. Which of the following is the most compelling argument for cyberspace governance?

The proliferation of internationalized cybercrime.	40%
The incidence of "political" cyber attacks (e.g. pro-nationalist hackers).	8%
The impact of cyber activity on foreign and military policy.	23%
The possibility of a cyber "arms race" in the near future.	22%
Other	7%

TOPIC 5: AFGHANISTAN AND IRAQ

ISSUE A. With the killing of Osama bin Laden and other key terrorist leaders, al-Qaeda has lost momentum and is on the wane.

Strongly agree	4%
Agree	47%
Disagree	43%
Strongly disagree	6%

ISSUE B. In your opinion, what is the most compelling reason for a continued U.S. presence in Afghanistan? (Select one)

It is critical to thwart the Taliban and terrorist groups seeking sanctuary in Afghanistan.	24%
Considering the strained nature of U.S.-Pakistan relations, Afghanistan is essential to curbing Pakistani extremists.	27%
The U.S. has an obligation to assist the Afghan government in stabilizing the country.	31%
Other	19%

ISSUE C. The U.S. should increase its efforts to stem the flow of insurgents, their matériel, and support from Pakistan into Afghanistan.

Strongly agree	23%
Agree	49%
Disagree	23%
Strongly disagree	5%

ISSUE D. Following the Obama Administration's 2011 deadline for the exit of U.S. troops from Iraq, how should the U.S. best view Iraq?

As a strategic partner in the war on terrorism.	9%
As a regional counterweight to the threat of a nuclear Iran.	22%
As a potential area for economic investment and development.	17%
As a fledgling democracy that requires assistance.	45%
Other	7%

TOPIC 6: OCEANS

ISSUE A. The U.S. should ratify the UN Convention on the Law of the Sea.

Yes	79%
No, the U.S.'s current status as a non-ratifying signatory is sufficient	8%
No, and the U.S. should not be a signatory to the treaty	3%
Not sure	10%

ISSUE B. In your opinion, which of the following is the most pressing ocean policy issue?

Undersea minerals and other natural resources	11%
Transit and shipping access	6%
Sustainability of fish stocks	41%
Rising sea levels	14%
Loss of biodiversity	17%
Claims on the Arctic	5%
Other	6%

ISSUE C. Issues of fisheries management are best handled through:

International organizations like the UN	57%
Local/regional governance	32%
Individual nations	11%

ISSUE D. The U.S. and other countries with sovereignty in the Arctic region should negotiate an agreement similar to the Antarctic Treaty.

Strongly agree	49%
Agree	46%
Disagree	5%
Strongly disagree	1%

TOPIC 7: INDONESIA

ISSUE A. Indonesia has completed the process of democratization and no longer needs assistance from the U.S. or the international community.

Strongly agree	3%
Agree	33%
Disagree	57%
Strongly disagree	7%

ISSUE B. Relative to other allies in Southeast Asia (Japan, South Korea and Taiwan), the U.S. should prioritize relations with Indonesia.

Strongly agree	9%
Agree	58%
Disagree	31%
Strongly disagree	2%

ISSUE C. Expansion of U.S.-Indonesia relations should focus on which issue?

Trade and economic development	39%
Global terrorism	5%
Regional stability in Southeast Asia	46%
Combating China's influence	9%
Other	2%

TOPIC 8: ENERGY GEOPOLITICS

ISSUE A. Constructing the Keystone XL pipeline is in the U.S. national interest.

Strongly agree	20%
Agree	37%
Disagree	30%
Strongly disagree	13%

ISSUE B. The most appropriate way for the U.S. to ensure its energy security is:

Supply-side: Secure imported energy supplies	4%
Supply-side: Develop alternative, more efficient energy supplies	57%
Demand-side: Reduce domestic consumption of energy	27%
Other	12%

ISSUE C. Russian exploration in the Arctic is a threat to U.S. interests.

Yes	48%
No	18%
Not sure	34%

ISSUE D. The U.S. should ratify the Kyoto Protocol.

Strongly agree	37%
Agree	42%
Disagree	16%
Strongly disagree	6%

Copies of the **National Opinion Ballot Report** *are available upon request. The* **NOBR** *is also available at* **www.fpa.org** *as a PDF.*

Global Discussion Questions

No decision in foreign policy is made in a vacuum, and the repercussions of any single decision have far-reaching effects across the range of strategic interests on the U.S. policy agenda. This GREAT DECISIONS feature is intended to facilitate the discussion of this year's topics in a global context, to discuss the linkages between the topics and to encourage consideration of the broader impact of decisionmaking.

---

1. Consider "China in Africa" and "Myanmar and Southeast Asia." How can outside nations help to accelerate development? Are there risks associated with outside involvement? What are the opportunities and advantages that make development and foreign investment attractive to governments of developing nations? What are the links to natural resource wealth? Why did Myanmar's government halt the Chinese dam project, whereas African governments have been more welcoming of Chinese development projects?

2. Consider "NATO" in the context of "Future of the euro." In terms of security, the economy and global politics, is the U.S. pulling away from Europe or becoming more integrated? Are U.S. interests aligned with European interests? If so, which ones?

3. Consider "Egypt" in the context of "Myanmar and Southeast Asia." What common challenges face these countries in their transition to full democracy? How did democratic reforms begin in each country, and how do these origins shape the path that each country will take? To what extent has the old order accepted change in each case, and to what extent will it be a part of the new order?

4. In the cases of "Iran" and "Myanmar and Southeast Asia," the U.S. and the West imposed sanctions for different reasons. Iran, with its nuclear ambitions, presents a security threat that Myanmar does not. Consider the effect of sanctions in each case. Is Myanmar a success story that proves the effectiveness of sanctions? What factors have made sanctions less fruitful in the case of Iran?

5. In "Egypt," popular revolution has given way to a messy struggle between competing interests—the military, Islamist parties, liberals—as democracy dawns on the country. Compare this case with "Myanmar," where the regime, not a popular uprising, ushered in change. Is popular support for regime change sufficient and necessary? Are parts of an old regime more or less likely to survive if they initiate democratic reform?

6. Consider "Future of the euro" in the context of "Threat assessment." Why does economic crisis put nations into such dire risk? Is this kind of threat a new one that is the product of increased international integration (e.g. monetary union)? How do enconomic entangle-ments—such as the U.S. with China, or the euro zone countries with each other—widen the potential effects of economic behavior and misbehavior?

7. Consider the history of allied operations in "NATO" and the evolution of the responsibil-ity to protect doctrine in "Intervention." Is R2P one of NATO's responsibilities? Is NATO, as a regional body with limited membership, endowed with the authority and the capability for effective intervention, or is intervention best left to the United Nations?

8. "Egypt" discusses the debate about the place that Islam should have in government, as well as the growing political power of the Muslim Brotherhood and the conservative Salafists. In "Iran," on the other hand, democratic institutions and theocratic ones are inter-twined. Do Egyptian politics seem as though they might follow an Iranian-style trajectory? Why or why not? What features of society or of government allow religious conservatives to gain political power?

9. In light of the threats outlined in "Threat assessment," how should the U.S. prioritize "NATO," "Iran," "Intervention" and "Future of the euro"?

10. In the context of "Intervention," did Myanmar's refusal of humanitarian aid after Cy-clone Nargis, as described in "Myanmar and Southeast Asia," provide sufficient grounds to invoke the responsibility to protect doctrine? Why or why not?

Headline Series

SINCE **1935,** the Foreign Policy Association has published over 3 million issues of the insightful and concise *Headline Series*. The roster of over 330 authors represents a who's who of foreign policy experts and leading journalists. Each issue of the pocket-size *Headline Series* is devoted to a single geographic area or topic of global concern. Recent titles include *The Persian Gulf: Tradition and Transformation* and *The Quest for African Unity.'*

Available as single copies, these inexpensive, succinct and well-researched books demystify the complexities of international affairs. Many provide background for **Great Decisions** topics.

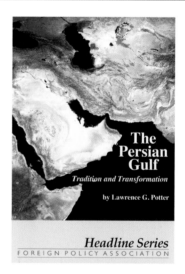

HEADLINE SERIES No. 332
Published Fall 2010
$8.99 plus S&H
ISBN# 978-0-87124-225-7; ID# 31594

collaboration
a word that allows us to grow together

Ilana Yahav
for eni

we work in more than 80 countries to bring you energy

eni
eni.com

Become a member

Associate—$250
Benefits:
- Free admission to all Associate events (includes member's family)
- Discounted admission for all other guests to Associate events
- Complimentary GREAT DECISIONS briefing book

National Associate*—$75
Benefits:
- Complimentary issue of FPA's annual *National Opinion Ballot Report* and GREAT DECISIONS Updates

*Residents of New York, New Jersey and Connecticut are not eligible.

Student—$50
Benefits:
- Free admission to all Associate events
- Discounted foreign policy publications
- Complimentary issue of FPA's annual *National Opinion Ballot Report*

FOREIGN POLICY ASSOCIATION 1918

Make a donation
Your support helps the FOREIGN POLICY ASSOCIATION'S *programs dedicated to global affairs education.*

Make a fully tax-deductible contribution to FPA's Annual Fund 2013.

To contribute to the Annual Fund 2013, contact an individual-giving specialist by calling the Membership Department at **(800) 628-5754 ext. 232,** or by visiting us online at **www.fpa.org**.

The generosity of donors who contribute $500 or more is acknowledged in FPA's *Annual Report.*

All financial contributions are tax-deductible to the fullest extent of the law under section 501 (c)(3) of the IRS code.

FPA also offers membership at the SPONSOR ASSOCIATE and PATRON ASSOCIATE levels. To learn more, contact the Membership Department at (800) 628-5754, ext. 232.

Return this form by mail to: Foreign Policy Association, 470 Park Avenue South, New York, N.Y. 10016.
Or fax to: (212) 481-9275.

TO ORDER FPA PUBLICATIONS: (800) 477-5836

ORDER ONLINE: WWW.GREATDECISIONS.ORG

FOR MEMBERSHIP CALL (800) 628-5754 EXT. 232

❑ MR.   ❑ MRS.   ❑ MS.   ❑ DR.   ❑ PROF.

NAME _____

ADDRESS _____

_____**APT/FLOOR** _____

CITY _____ **STATE** _____ **ZIP** _____

TEL _____

E-MAIL _____

❑ AMEX   ❑ VISA   ❑ MC   ❑ DISCOVER
❑ CHECK (ENCLOSED)

CHECKS SHOULD BE PAYABLE TO FOREIGN POLICY ASSOCIATION.

CARD NO.

SIGNATURE OF CARDHOLDER

EXP. DATE (MM/YY)

PRODUCT	QTY	PRICE	COST
GREAT DECISIONS 2013 TEACHER'S PACKET (1 Briefing Book, 1 Teacher's Guide & 1 DVD) E-MAIL: (REQUIRED) _____		$65	
GREAT DECISIONS 2013 CLASSROOM PACKET (1 Teacher's Packet & 30 Briefing Books) E-MAIL: (REQUIRED) _____		$460	
GREAT DECISIONS 2013 DVD		$40	
Headline Series Nos. 333-334, THE PERSIAN GULF: TRADITION AND TRANSFORMATION (Double issue)		$14.99	
ASSOCIATE MEMBERSHIP		$250	
NATIONAL ASSOCIATE MEMBERSHIP		$75	
STUDENT MEMBERSHIP		$50	
ANNUAL FUND 2013 (ANY AMOUNT)			

*For details and shipping charges, call FPA's Sales Department at (800) 477-5836.

Orders mailed to FPA without the shipping charge will be held.

SUBTOTAL $ _____

plus S & H* $ _____

TOTAL $ _____